PAUL'S DOCTRINE OF
REDEMPTION

THE MACMILLAN COMPANY
NEW YORK · BOSTON · CHICAGO
DALLAS · ATLANTA · SAN FRANCISCO

MACMILLAN & CO., Limited
LONDON · BOMBAY · CALCUTTA
MELBOURNE

THE MACMILLAN CO. OF CANADA, Ltd.
TORONTO

PAUL'S DOCTRINE OF REDEMPTION

BY

HENRY BEACH CARRÉ, B.D., Ph.D.

PROFESSOR OF BIBLICAL THEOLOGY AND ENGLISH
EXEGESIS, VANDERBILT UNIVERSITY

New York
THE MACMILLAN COMPANY
1914

61949

To My Wife and Mother

WHOSE JOINT SACRIFICE AND CO-OPERATION HAVE MADE
THESE PAGES POSSIBLE

PREFACE

In the preface to his recent book,[1] Schweitzer reaffirms the conclusion announced by him in his previous work,[2] which was that the proper understanding of Jesus is arrived at only by a thorough-going application to the interpretation of the Gospels of the principle of eschatology, based exclusively upon "the contemporary Apocalyptic." He believes that, in his faithful application of this principle to these sources, he has "created a new fact upon which to base the history of dogma."[3] The next task, he thinks, is to "define the position of Paul," which in this connection means to determine whether the Apostle to the Gentiles represents the "first stage of the Hellenizing process," which the history of dogma

[1] Schweitzer, *Geschichte der paulinischen Forschung,* Tübingen, 1911. Eng. tr., *Paul and His Interpreters. A Critical History,* London, 1912.

[2] Schweitzer, *von Reimarus zu Wrede,* Tübingen. 1906. Eng. tr., *The Quest of the Historical Jesus,* London, 1910.

[3] *Geschichte der paulinischen Forschung,* p. viii. Eng. tr., p. ix.

discloses, or whether Paul is essentially at one with the Jewish-eschatological thought of primitive Christianity. He thinks the latter alternative to be the correct one, and, in view of it, promises the public within a short time a "new formulation of the problem of Paulinism," under the title, "The Pauline Mysticism."

The important place given to eschatology by Schweitzer will doubtless help materially to our understanding of Paul, but it will not of itself furnish the solution of the problem which Paulinism presents to the historical interpreter. Eschatology was only one item in Paul's thought, albeit a very important one. It has to do with a great catastrophic event in the near future and with important and far-reaching cosmic happenings connected therewith.

While it is evident that Paul thought of all things as moving toward this eschatological moment, it is also clear that, as far as men were concerned, the future life was irrevocably conditioned on what transpired in this life. It is essential, therefore, that one present the eschatology of Paul as being of a piece with his entire world philosophy. It grows out of, and is the

logical sequel to, all that has gone before. To
look at the end without having regard to the
beginning as well as to the period between the
beginning and the end is to misunderstand Paul.

The present study is an attempt to interpret
the Apostle from the standpoint of his world
philosophy. We believe that we have given to
eschatology its proper proportion and significance, while, at the same time, we have under-
taken to show that the redemption of man, as
Paul conceived it, was inseparably connected
with the redemption of the cosmos, and that the
same principles which underlie the world's redemption are at work in the redemption of mankind. Man's salvation is a chapter of cosmical
history, as it unfolded itself to the dualism of
Paul.

A word touching the manner of treatment.
Only here and there, and that incidentally, have
we indicated the probable extra-Biblical sources
of Paul's ideas. The question touching the
sources of Paul's ideas is a large one, and the
materials for its study are as yet in a chaotic
condition. However, enough is already known
to leave no room for doubt that Paul did his

work in a highly syncretic environment. This fact, taken along with his mental alertness and his highly sensitive nature, makes it very probable that he was, in no small degree, influenced by the strong thought-currents of his day.

No attempt has been made to determine the significance of the sacraments for the Pauline soteriology. The problem of the sacraments is complex and connected with the one just mentioned. It requires extended treatment. Its omission has not materially affected, we believe, our results. The sacraments had to do in some way with the appropriation of salvation by the believer. They did not affect the fact of salvation, or determine the means through which it was achieved by the Redeemer. It is with these latter questions that we are most concerned in this investigation.

The present discussion is based almost exclusively upon the ten more generally accepted letters of Paul, which are regarded as alike Pauline. For purposes of comparison a few references have been made to the Pastorals. The use of the Pauline material is not indicative of the writer's views touching special questions of authorship. At the same time, he has been careful to see that every important conclusion is adequately supported by the well attested letters of Paul. It is worthy of notice that the interpretation of the leading ideas of these unquestioned letters from the standpoint of cosmology has disclosed a greater homogeneity of thought underlying them and the so-called Christological letters, than it is customary· to recognize. If this fact has any bearing on the problems of New Testament Introduction, it is an indirect and unintended result of this study.

The writer desires to thank the members of the Faculty of the New Testament Department of the University of Chicago for many helpful courtesies. Especially to Professor C. W. Votaw is he indebted for invaluable aid both in the preparation of the manuscript and in the reading of the proof.

For the compiling of the Index of Scripture References the author is indebted to his wife.

HENRY BEACH CARRÉ.

Chicago, Ill.,.August, 1913.

TABLE OF CONTENTS.

CHAPTER I

THE WORLD-VIEW OF PAUL

PAUL had a philosophy of the universe, which
went back to the beginning of things, and accounted for the existence of the world. At one
with the Jewish thought of his day on this point,[4]
he regarded the world as God's creation.[5] As a
Christian, he went beyond this, and conceived of
Christ as being, in some undescribed way, the
Creator of all things.[6] Paul's philosophy was
practical, not speculative. He was not, so far
as his letters show, greatly interested in the meta-
physical and speculative questions regarding the
origin of the universe of matter, with which

[4] See Bousset, *Die Religion des Judentums im neutestamentlichen Zeitalter,* Berlin, 2 Aufl., 1906, 410 f.

[5] Rom. 1:25; 8:20; Eph. 3:9.

[6] Col. 1:15-20. It is perhaps not permissible to limit
"All things" (v. 16) to the spiritual beings enumerated
here. But their enumeration and the omission of any
reference to the world of matter points strongly to the
probability that the important point of difference between
Paul and the false teachers at Colosse had to do with
the relation of Christ to these world-powers.

philosophy, that of his day and that of later
times, has been concerned. He was interested
in man's redemption from the evils of the present
world and in his eternal blessedness.

His interest in the cosmos[7] took its start from
those events that occasioned the misfortunes
from which man needs to be saved. His interest
ended with those happenings in the future which
mark the final stages in the redemptive program.
With the Parousia, the Resurrection of the
Saints, the Judgment, and those events that were

[7] The sense in which the word cosmos ($\kappa\acute{o}\sigma\mu o\varsigma$) is
used in this investigation is a well-established usage in
Paul. He views the cosmos from two standpoints. At
times he thinks of the material universe, the world of
matter (Rom. 1:20; 1 Cor. 3:22; 8:4; Eph. 1:4). Again
he has in mind more particularly the world of intelli-
gences which inhabit the cosmos. These include (a)
men whose abode is the earth, (b) intermediary beings,
who inhabit both the lower and the superterrestrial
regions (Rom. 3:6; 1 Cor. 4:9; 6:2, 3; Col. 2:20, with
"elements"). It is not always possible to tell with certainty just what particular meaning Paul has in mind. It
may be possible to include other passages in the lists
given. In addition to these two significations, which are
the ones of most concern to us in this study, Paul uses
the word cosmos for the earth proper (Rom. 1:8; Col.
1:6; 2:20, with "living in"), also for the inhabitants of
the world, or human society (Rom. 3:19; 4:13; 1 Cor.
1:27 f; 5:10; 14:10) and for men as estranged from
God, i. e., the wicked (1 Cor. 1:21; 2 Cor. 7:10).

connected with it, the curtain falls. Beyond that, Paul contents himself with one all-inclusive assurance, namely, that God will "be all in all," [8] and that he will exercise over the cosmos an eternal sway, which shall not be disputed.

Looking back over the earlier chapters of the cosmic history, of which eschatology is only the final chapter, we find, with Paul as our guide, that there has been in progress, from the beginning, a cosmic struggle for the mastery of the universe. The combatants in this contest are, on the one side, God and all that is good; on the other side, Satan and all that is evil. This last named group includes Satan's host of demonic beings, as well as those men, who, by their indulgence in sin, have allied themselves with Satan and his hosts, and have, by so doing, become his allies and in consequence the enemies of God.[9] Satan's opponent was the God of the

---

[8] 1 Cor. 15:28.

[9] In referring to the evil powers, Paul uses a variety of terms. He seems to have no fixed conception of the relation of these powers to each other and to the cosmos. He is not concerned with angelology for its own sake. For him demonic sway over the world constituted a hiatus in the world process. He shows himself familiar

Hebrews, the God of Paul's inherited faith, the only real God, the living God, who had created the heavens and the earth. Satan [10] was the adversary, not alone of men's souls, but of God himself and of God's order and rule.[11] His opposition to God was not theoretical, passive or intermittent, but actual, active and constant. It had been of long duration and had been, through-

with it, and recognizes its reality; but, since this entire demonic host is shortly to be overthrown, it can only have a passing interest. This interest, however, is intensely real while it lasts, because these beings are actual antagonists, not only of God, but also of every individual; and they must be overcome, if the future blessings are to be enjoyed. Paul uses the following names: Satan, Belial, the Evil One, the Tempter, the Serpent, the Devil, the God of this Age, the Ruler of the Power of the Air, the Spirit that now works in the sons of disobedience, Demons, Spirits, Gods, Lords, Elements, the Rulers of this Age, Principalities, Authorities, Powers, Angels, Dominions. On Death and Sin see pp. 26-32.

[10] Despite the elasticity observed in Paul's use of terms referring to the cosmic foes of God, and despite the further fact that the form of the Devil is not prominent in Paul (noted by Bousset, *Religion des Judentums*, 2 Aufl., Berlin, 1906, who also cites J. Weiss, *Realencyclopädie*, 3 Aufl., 409 f. and Everling) while the demons play a large part, it nevertheless is clear that Paul, in common with post-exilic Judaism, regarded the chief of the demonic hosts, namely, the Devil, Satan, or Belial, as the cosmic foe of God *par éminence*.

[11] I Cor. 15:24-28.

out its length, fierce in the extreme.[12]   It was
war to the finish, no quarter to be given.[13]

[12] Bousset, *Religion des Judentums,* 2 Aufl., Berlin, 1906,
289 ff.

[13] The place of angelology and demonology in the
thought of Paul has for the most part been overlooked by
interpreters.   The first to give it thorough-going scientific treatment was Everling, *Die paulinische Angelologie
und Dämonologie,* Göttingen, 1888.   Prior to Everling,
others had given the question consideration in works of
a general character: Gfrörer, *Das Jahrhundert des
Heils,* Stuttgart, 1838; Hilgenfeld, *Der Galaterbrief,* Leipzig, 1852; Klöpper, *Der Brief an die Colosser,* Berlin,
1882; Spitta, *Der zweite Brief des Petrus und der Brief
des Judas,* Halle, 1885.   After Everling, the next to give
the subject careful examination was Kabisch, *Die Eschatologie des Paulus in ihren Zusammenhängen mit dem
Gesamtbegriff des Paulinismus,* Göttingen, 1893; Wernle,
Die Anfänge unserer Religion, Tübingen und Leipzig,
1901, 2 Aufl., 1904; English translation of first edition,
The Beginnings of Christianity, London and New York,
1903.   Wernle directed attention to the importance of
demonology in the Pauline Soteriology, but failed to make
thorough use of the idea.   The first one to make the
attempt really to interpret Paul's Christology from the
standpoint of the cosmic struggle was Brückner, *Die
Entstehung der paulinischen Christologie,* Strassburg,
1903; followed by Wrede, *Paulus,* Tübingen, 1904.   Next
came Dibelius, *Die Geisterwelt im Glauben des Paulus,*
Göttingen, 1909.   Dibelius builds upon the work of Everling, but carries it forward chiefly in three directions:
(1) He makes larger use of rabbinic material than did
Everling; (2) he undertakes a more thorough-going explanation of the origin of Paul's ideas; (3) he endeav-
ors to show the significance, for Paul's faith, of his
ideas regarding the world of spirits.   Everling did not

Thus far Satan had had the better of the contest. First, he had triumphed in that critical moment of cosmic history, when the first pair were put on trial. Their disobedience was a temporary defeat for God. God had a right to expect that Adam would be true to him, and stand the test successfully. Had he done so, mankind would have escaped the ills from which it has since suffered. The demonic powers would have exercised no influence on the earth, or in the affairs of men.[14] As it turned out, however, an innumerable host of invisible enemies was turned

attempt to show the significance of angelology and demonology for the faith of Paul. Dibelius regards this as a fault in Everling's book, and as the reason why his results were for a while given slight attention, as Brückner observes, p. 192. Dibelius further observes that the older conception did not regard the investigation of Paul's views regarding the world of spirits as of value, because it had nothing to do with the real faith of Paul. The first of these two propositions, he holds, Everling has completely disproved. Regarding the second, he maintains that belief in the world of spirits is of special importance for the Eschatology and the Christology of Paul. To overlook these facts is to lose a "portion" (*Stück*) of Paul's faith (pp. 4 f). Dibelius himself, however, does not recognize that demonology had much to do with Paul's leading religious ideas (p. 191).

[14] This is the natural inference from Rom. 5:12-21; 6:23; 1 Cor. 15:21, 22.

loose to work their will upon men, who, in their limited, human strength, were wholly incapable of coping with them. This was not surprising. These powers, or their chief, at least, had temporarily triumphed over God. How could man then hope to prevail against them?

Of this vast host of hostile forces, the two which were of most concern to men were sin and death. It was sin that took advantage of the prohibition to Adam and Eve, and, through their disobedience of God's command, entered into human affairs. But sin did not come alone. Along with sin there came, both as companion and as finisher of his work, that most dreaded of all man's foes—death.[15]

[15] In 2 Cor. 11:3, Paul says that in his craftiness the serpent deceived Eve. Cf. 1 Tim. 2:14 f. Paul's custom, however, would seem to be to attribute the Fall to Adam, Rom. 5:12-21; 1 Cor. 15:21, 22. See Gen. 2:16, 17; 3:1-24. Both traditions obtained in Jewish theology. "From a woman was the beginning of sin; And because of her we all die." (*Ecclesiasticus* 25:24.) The rabbis had much to say regarding Eve as the cause of Man's fall. See citations by Weber, *Altsynagogale Theologie,* Leipzig, 1880, 210 ff. As a rule, however, the Fall was attributed to Adam: "And unto him thou gavest commandment to love thy way: which he transgressed, and immediately thou appointedst death in him and in his genera-

In speaking of sin and death it is necessary to observe that Paul did not think of sin and death altogether as the modern man thinks of them. He looked upon each of these human experiences from two different standpoints. From one standpoint his view does not differ very much from our own. With us, he regards sin as a transgression of law, an attitude of rebellion, or insubordination to the authority of God.[16] He spoke also of sinning against one's brother.[17] Likewise he used the word death as we do. It may mean simply physical death, the death

tions, of whom came nations, tribes, peoples, and kindreds, out of number. And every people walked after their own will, and did wonderful things before thee, and despised thy commandments." (IV Ezra 3:7.) "Because for their sakes I made the world: and when Adam transgressed my statutes, then was decreed that now is done. Then were the entrances of this world made narrow, full of sorrow and travail: they are but few and evil, full of perils, and very painful." (IV Ezra 7:11, 12.) "O thou Adam, what hast thou done? for though it was thou that sinned, thou art not fallen alone, but we all that came of thee." (IV Ezra 7:118.)

[16] In this sense Paul usually uses the verb sin: Rom. 2:12; 3:23; 5:12, 14, 16; 6:15; 1 Cor. 7:28, 36; 15:34, and the substantives, transgression Rom. 5:14, misdeed Rom. 4:25; 5:15-18, 20, and sin, evil deed, Rom. 3:25; 1 Cor. 6:18.

[17] 1 Cor. 8:9-13.

of the body.[18]   It may mean the loss of eternal
life.[19]   In these usages, the terms, sin and death,
have a natural significance, which we find no difficulty in determining.   Sin is regarded as a
psychic phenomenon, having to do with volition
and action in relation to others.   Death is viewed
as a universal phenomenon in the material world,
or in a metaphorical sense, referring to a future
condition, which is for our thought analogous to
the physical phenomenon with which we are
familiar.

But there is another standpoint from which
Paul viewed sin and death.   It is extremely difficult, if indeed possible, for the modern man to
stand with him at this point of vision, and con-
template them as he did.   Yet it is absolutely
necessary to the understanding of Paul that, to a
certain extent, one accustom himself to Paul's
mode of thought in this respect.   It must not be
imagined, however, that Paul originated this
manner of thinking or that he to any extent
monopolized it.   He was by no means unique at
this point, but was thoroughly a man of his

[18] Phil. 1:20; 2:27, 30.
[19] 2 Cor. 2:16; 7:10.

times.[20] It goes without saying that he not only used the vocabulary of his day, but also the thought-forms of his day. Otherwise, the first readers of his epistles would have had as much difficulty in understanding him as theologians have had from that day to the present.

For several centuries preceding the age of Paul, how much earlier we do not know, and for a considerable time thereafter, men were accustomed to refer to a given phenomenon and to its cause, by the use of the same word. In applying the term to the phenomenon itself, apart from any thought of its cause, their mental process was not unlike our own. They used the words wisdom, reason, law, sin, death, and other words in much the same way that we do, that is, as terms corresponding with certain concepts, whether abstract or concrete.

On the other hand, they used these same terms much as we do proper names. They apparently thought of wisdom,[21] reason, [22] and the like as entities, as actual living existences, or beings.

[20] Charles, *Book of Enoch,* 2d Ed. Oxford, 1912, CIV f.
[21] Prov. 8:22-31; Job 28; Clem. Alex., Strom. VI, 7.
[22] Clem. Alex., *Exhortation to the Heathen,* Ch. I.

Paul speaks of sin [23] and death,[23] and, as shown
later, of law,[24] as though they were sentient beings. Sin [25] and Death [25] are said to enter into
the world. They are said to reign as sovereigns.
Death passes unto or upon all men. Men die to
Sin; live in Sin; are the slaves of Sin. These
and kindred expressions would, in ordinary cases,
indicate a personification of these ideas. Interpreters as a rule so understand them.[26] It will

[23] Rom., Chaps. 5, 6, 7.

[24] Pp. 69-71.

[25] From this point on capitals are used with these words
when the personal significance here referred to is present
in them.

[26] See Thayer, *Lexicon;* Jülicher, in J. Weiss, *Die Schriften des Neuen Testaments,* 2 Aufl., Göttingen, 1908, II,
256, 264, 271. Sanday feels that Paul's language in Rom.,
Chaps. 6, 7, does not carry us beyond personification, yet
he recognizes that personification does not adequately
explain Paul's thought, and that a "personal agency"
must in some way be predicated. His indecision is noteworthy: "And although it is doubtless true that in chaps.
VI, VII, where Paul speaks most directly of the baleful
activity of Sin, he does not intend to lay special stress
on this; his language is of the nature of personification
and does not necessarily imply a person; yet when we
take it in connection with other language elsewhere [i. e.,
in the Corinthian, Ephesian, Colossian, Thessalonian, and
Pastoral Epistles], we see that in the last resort he would
have said that there was a personal agency at work. It is
at least clear that he is speaking of an influence external
to man, and acting upon him in a way in which spiritual
forces act. . . . He too expresses truth through symbols,

be developed more fully in the course of this study that Paul's language carries us quite beyond the rhetorical device of personification. The thorough-going investigations of Everling,[27] Kabisch [28] and Dibelius [29] leave little room for doubt that with Paul Sin and Death were, from a certain point of view, hypostases, existences, beings, or personalities. As such, they are to be classed along with the Principalities, Powers, Rulers, Angels, Demons, and the rest of that innumerable host of cosmic beings which, as we have already seen, constituted a prime factor in Paul's world problem.

We have already observed that Paul's philosophy was practical, not academic. He was decidedly more interested in man's fate than he

and in the days when men can dispense with symbols his teaching may be obsolete, but not before." Note on "St. Paul's Conception of Sin and the Fall," in *International Critical Commentary on the Epistle to the Romans,* New York, 1895, pp. 145-147. In justification of Sanday's reluctance to concede anything beyond a personification of sin in Rom., Chaps. 6, 7, may be noted the use of human law with the verb, to rule (7:1).

[27] *Die paulinische Angelologie und Dämonologie,* Göttingen, 1888.

[28] *Die Eschatologie des Paulus,* Göttingen, 1893.

[29] *Die Geisterwelt im Glauben des Paulus,* Göttingen, 1909.

was in the construction of an Apocalyptist's cosmology. We do not find him running off into endless speculation regarding the inhabitants of the lower regions and of the super-terrestrial regions. He was chiefly concerned with those two particular cosmic forces, or beings, that had most to do with man's present and future misery, namely, Sin and Death. In this intensely practical character of his philosophy we probably have an explanation of the striking fact already referred to, that he has relatively little to say regarding the chief of the cosmic foes of God and of man, namely, the Devil, or Satan. As Paul saw it, the cosmic struggle under which the world was groaning was not primarily a struggle between the Devil and his hosts, on the one side, and men on the other, but a struggle between the Devil and his hosts, on one side, and God on the other. Satan and God—these were the protagonists. Man played a secondary part. He was drawn into the cosmic drama by no act of his own, but by an accident, or misfortune, in the yielding of the first pair to the seductions of Satan, God's enemy. By their disobedience to their Creator they fell into the power of this adversary of God, their punishment being that they and their progeny should be at the mercy of two of Satan's subordinates, namely, Sin and Death. It was these two subordinates of the chief adversary with which man had most to do. It is not surprising, therefore, that Paul has comparatively little to say regarding the Devil, while Sin and Death bulk large in his writings. Nor is it surprising that, at the thought of the overthrow of these demonic powers, he should exclaim: "O Death, where is thy victory? O Death, where is thy sting? The sting of Death is Sin; and the power of Sin is the Law: but thanks be to God, who giveth us the victory through our Lord, Jesus Christ!" [30]   As twin despots they had ruled supreme over men with relentless obstinacy and cruelty. From the hour of Adam's Fall, none had escaped their fury. Under their dominion, Jew and Gentile alike had plunged into the deepest depths of degradation and shame. In all the world there was not one good, no, not one! [31]   God had been driven from the field. Man was left helpless in the hands of

[30] I Cor. 15:55-57. Cf., Rom. 7:24, 25; 11:25-36.
[31] Rom. 1:18—3:20.

implacable and resistless foes. The cosmos languished under the sway of an imperial host of superhuman fiends.

Paul's philosophy could not leave humanity in the condition to which Sin and Death had brought it. His faith in God required that the sway of Satan and his hosts over the earth and the affairs of men should some day come to an end, and that God should rule supreme.[32] In accordance with this belief, the history of the cosmos was divided into two periods, eons, or ages, namely, the present age, and the coming age.[33] This division was more than a temporal one. The present age belonged to the evil spirits.[34] They ruled over it as sovereigns, dom-

[32] See citations in Dibelius, *Die Geisterwelt im Glauben des Paulus,* Göttingen, 1909, 100 f., and Kabisch, *Die Eschatologie des Paulus,* Göttingen, 1893.

[33] Rom. 12:2; 1 Cor. 1:20; 2:6, 8; 3:18; 2 Cor. 4:4; Gal. 1:4; Eph. 1:21; 2:2, 7; 6:12. This division of cosmic history was common in New Testament times, and in post-exilic Judaism. See Bousset, *Religion des Judentums,* 2 Aufl., Berlin, 1906, 321-324. Volz, *Jüdische Eschatologie,* Tübingen und Leipzig, 1903, 296-298. Schürer, *Geschichte des jüdischen Volkes,* 4 Aufl., Leipzig, 1907, II. 636 ff.

[34] The thought of the Graeco-Roman world of Paul's day was not materially different from that of Jewish theology with respect to the dominating influence in life

inating and controlling it to the extent that all phenomena which were adverse to man's interest and welfare were caused by them. Among these phenomena were reckoned diseases, especially such as produced striking abnormality, as lunacy, epilepsy, paralysis. Other of these phenomena were storms, droughts, lightning, thunder, and the various ills of humanity, last and chief of all —death. Man lived in a continuous fear of these foes of his happiness. Life was one long attempt to avoid displeasing them. It was an "evil age." To escape from it would be the greatest possible blessing and happiness.

The coming age, on the contrary, belonged unquestionably to God. Good must triumph over evil. Ultimately, God, who had been, for the most part, dispossessed of the cosmos, which he had created, would assert his sway over it by subduing or destroying the hosts of Satan that had for so long usurped its control. This optimism Paul expresses frequently, but notably in the two following passages:

of the evil spirits and the desire for salvation from their power and control. See Bousset, in J. Weiss, *Die Schriften des Neuen Testaments,* Göttingen, 1908, II, 32 f.

"But now hath Christ been raised from the dead, the first fruits of them that are asleep. For since by man came Death, by man came also the resurrection of the dead. For as in Adam all die, so also in Christ shall all be made alive. But each in his own order: Christ the first fruits; then they that are Christ's, at his coming. Then cometh the end, when he shall deliver up the kingdom to God, even the Father; when he shall have abolished all rule and all authority and power. For he must reign, till he hath put all his enemies under his feet. The last enemy that shall be abolished is Death. For, He put all things in subjection under his feet. But when he saith, All things are put in subjection, it is evident that he is excepted who did subject all things unto him. And when all things have been subjected unto him, then shall the Son also himself be subjected to him that did subject all things unto him, that God may be all in all." [35]

"For I reckon that the sufferings of this present time are not worthy to be compared with the glory which shall be revealed to usward. For the earnest expectation of the creation waiteth

[35] I Cor. 15:20-28.

for the revealing of the sons of God. For the creation was subjected to vanity, not of its own will, but by reason of him who subjected it, in hope that the creation itself also shall be delivered from the bondage of corruption into the liberty of the glory of the children of God. For we know that the whole creation groaneth and travaileth in pain together until now. And not only so, but ourselves also, who have the first-fruits of the Spirit, even we ourselves groan within ourselves, waiting for our adoption, to wit, the redemption of our body. . . . And we know that to them that love God all things work together for good, even to them that are called according to his purpose. For whom he foreknew, he also foreordained to be conformed to the image of his Son, that he might be the first born among many brethren: and whom he foreordained, them he also called: and whom he called, them he also justified; and whom he justified, them he also glorified. What then shall we say to these things? If God is for us, who is against us? He that spared not his own Son, but delivered him up for us all, how shall he not also with him freely give us all things? Who shall

lay anything to the charge of God's elect? It is
God that justifieth; who is he that condemneth?
It is Christ Jesus that died, yea, rather, that was
raised from the dead, who is at the right hand of
God, who also maketh intercession for us. Who
shall separate us from the love of Christ? shall
tribulation, or anguish, or persecution, or famine,
or nakedness, or peril, or sword? Even as it is
written,

> For thy sake we are killed all the day long;
> We were accounted as sheep for the slaughter.

Nay, in all these things we are more than conquerors through him that loved us. For I am
persuaded, that neither death, nor life, nor angels,
nor principalities, nor things present, nor things
to come, nor powers, nor height, nor depth, nor
any other creature, shall be able to separate us
from the love of God, which is in Christ Jesus
our Lord." [36]

From the foregoing it is evident that the division of the history of the cosmos into two great
periods of time, a present and a future age, had
for its basis the dualistic philosophy which was

[36] Rom. 8:18-39.

common in the time of Paul, among both Jews and Greeks. These two periods were characterized by the sway of two great cosmic forces, which were totally opposed to each other. When either of these forces was in control of the world, the other must be, to a large extent, if not entirely, quiescent or ineffective. The present age with all its evil must give way to the coming age, which will be filled with every conceivable good.

In the light of all these facts we here lay down four propositions as being fundamental to a proper interpretation of Paul, and which will serve as guides to us in the remainder of this discussion:

1. *There must be a clear understanding of Paul's philosophy, including both his present world-view and his eschatology.*

2. *Paul's theology is not distinguishable from his philosophy, and therefore the salient features of his theology, so-called, are rooted in, and are one with his philosophy, or world-view.*

3. *Since Paul's theology interpreted the cosmos as being, in his time, under the control of the cosmic powers of evil, and just on the eve of*

momentous happenings which would eventuate in the transfer of its control to the cosmic forces of good, therefore, the Redemption of the World, according to Paul, means the overthrow of the evil cosmic powers and the enthronement of the good cosmic powers, or, in other words, the victory of God over Satan and his host of demons.

4. Since Paul was primarily interested in the practical rather than in the speculative side of this redemptive program of God, his scheme for human redemption is to be understood as a part of the cosmic redemption, i. e., as the freeing of man from the dominion of the demonic powers, in particular, Sin and Death.

CHAPTER II

LOOKED at through the eyes of Paul, the condition of the universe was not a happy one. The world, both of animate and of inanimate matter, groaned and travailed in pain, awaiting its deliverance from the Powers of Evil. It had been created by God capable of being made subject to these Powers, but with the purpose that it should be released ultimately from them, and given the freedom of the glory of the children of God. Men, in particular, groaned within themselves, confidently and momentarily expecting their final installation as sons of God, which carried with it the redemption of the body.[37]

It is evident that such phenomena as are here referred to were not to be expected as the result of a gradual or evolutionary process. The pic-

[37] Rom. 8:19-23. See also Rom. 1:18—3:18; 12:2; 1 Cor. 2:6; 2 Cor. 4:4; Eph. 2:2.

ture is of something sudden, cataclysmic, catastrophic. Moreover, the attitude of the cosmos,
man included, is that of relative passivity. The
contemplated changes are not predicated on the
basis of processes at work within the cosmos
but on the basis of an impending catastrophic
divine act. It is by waiting, expecting and being
prepared, that the blessings are to be secured.
The redemption is something to be wrought out
by God external to and for the benefit of the
cosmos. This applies as well to men as to inanimate matter. If Paul exhorted the Philippians to work out their own salvation with fear
and trembling, he immediately added: "For it
is God who works in you both to will and to
effect in you his good intention for you." [38] The
world is unable to save itself; it must have a
Redeemer or Savior from without.

The reason for this is to be found in the fact
that the foes in whose thraldom it is held are
superhuman foes. "For our conflict is not
against blood and flesh, but against the principalities, against the powers, against the world-

[38] Phil. 2:12, 13.

rulers of this darkness, against the spiritual hosts
of wickedness in the super-terrestrial regions."[39]
These foes are not going to relinquish their control over the world voluntarily. It must be taken
away from them by force. But this requires a
power stronger than they. There is but one such
Power and that is God. Man must rely on God,
the stronger Power, since of himself man can do
nothing.

While it is true, as will appear later, that
Christ is, from one point of view, the Redeemer,
it is also true that Paul conceives God the Father
to be ultimately the Redeemer of the cosmos.
To be sure, the gospel, which contains the plan
of redemption, is more frequently called the gos-
pel of Christ, but it is also the "gospel of God."[40]
Redemption is an expression of the love of
God.[41]   Eternal life is the free gift of God in
Christ Jesus, our Lord.[42]   It was God the Father

---

[39] Eph. 6:12. If one reads this entire passage, he will
be struck with two things: the completeness of the Christian's armor, or panoply, and the entire absence of sol-
dierly action. It is not the actual fighting, but the possession of the armor, which insures the victory.

[40] Rom. 1:1; 15:16; 2 Cor. 11:7; 1 Thes. 2:2, 8, 9.

[41] Rom. 5:7, 8; 8:39.

[42] Rom. 6:23.

who sent his Son to redeem men from Sin.[43]
God is on the side of men in their fight against
angels, principalities and powers.[44]   It was in
accordance with the will of God that Christ gave
himself for our sins, in order that he might deliver us from this present evil world.[45]   The
righteousness of God which is revealed in the
gospel is a condition of acceptance with God,[46]
which men enjoy by virtue of the fact that it
was a God-provided righteousness.   It had its
origin in God.   It was his grace, or love, that
provided it as his gift to men.[47]   It is the power
of God that is manifest in the gospel for the
salvation of men.[48]   God did not intend us to be
the victims of wrath, but the recipients of salvation through our Lord Jesus Christ.[49]

[43] Rom. 8: 3, 32.   Gal. 4:4.

[44] Rom. 8:31-39.

[45] Gal. 1:4.   " 'Deliver' strikes the key-note of the epistle.   The Gospel is a rescue, an emancipation, from a
state of bondage.   See esp. 4:9, 31; 5:1, 13."   Lightfoot,
Commentary on Galatians, London and Cambridge, 1869,
in loc.

[46] The genitive in the phrase, δικαιοσύνη θεοῦ, is one of
source.   This is uniform in Paul's usage of this phrase,
unless Rom. 3:5, 25, 26 be exceptions.   But see pp. 98-109.

[47] Rom. 3:24.

[48] Rom. 1:16.

[49] 1 Thes. 5:9.

We must next inquire more closely into the
character of the redemption, which God has effected for the world.   In this inquiry, the first
step will be to determine how Paul regarded the
two cosmic foes, with which man had most of
all to contend—Sin and Death.   The next step
will be to survey Paul's general conception of the
benefits which accrue to those who avail themselves of the salvation which God has provided.

Fundamentally there is no sharp distinction to
be drawn between Sin and Death, on the one
side, and their chief, Satan, on the other.   We
approach Paul's thought more nearly when we
regard Sin and Death as hypostases of Satan,
the same in being and purpose with him.   Jewish
demonology was at no time reduced to a well-
defined and fixed system, as to the particular
functions which the various demonic beings were
charged with.   Still there was a general classifi-
cation of them, from the standpoint of their
rank and of the service they performed.   But
this differentiation of them, the one from the
other, must not be thought of as a differentiation
of kind, or ultimately of person.   They were all
generically one.   In their unity they constituted

that primal evil power to which primitive peoples attribute all misfortune, sorrow and pain. In their differentiation they stood for the particular manifestation of that primal evil power that resulted in a given misfortune, or calamity. Death was closely united in thought with Satan, or the Devil. The author of the Epistle to the Hebrews interprets Christ's death as the means of destroying "him that hath the power of Death, that is, the Devil." [50] Paul attributes to Satan the power to destroy the body, that is, the power of Death.[51] The identification of Sin with the Devil seems to have been common in Paul's day. The haggadic literature substitutes the Devil for the serpent in the story of the Fall, or represents the Devil as assuming the form of a serpent.[52]

In Romans, chapters 5, 6, 7, we have Paul's most extended discussion of Sin. Rom. 5:12-21 is devoted to the theological side of the question.

[50] Heb. 2:14.

[51] I Cor. 5:5. Bousset regards Death, Hades, the angel of Hades, mentioned in Isa. 25:7 f., IV Ez. 8:53; Bar. 21:23; Tt. Levi 18; I Cor. 15:25 f., 55, as identical with the Devil. See also Dibelius, p. 115, and Kabisch, pp. 163 ff.

[52] See Bousset, *Die Religion des Judentums*, 2 Aufl., Berlin, 1906, 468 f.

Here the presence of Sin in the world is accounted for, as we have seen, by the Fall of
Adam. In chapters 6, 7 the ethical phase of the
question is considered. The actual workings of
Sin in human experience are depicted. Sin
reigns as a supreme sovereign in the mortal
bodies of unbelievers, compelling the desires to
obey it, and, in so doing, to commit transgressions against God.[53] Sin and God are lords bid
ding as it were for men's voluntary enslavement.[54] Men may choose as pleases them, now
that righteousness[55] has been provided in
Christ. [56] If they choose to enslave themselves

[53] Rom. 6:12-14.

[54] On the practice of voluntary enslavement to a deity
after liberation from literal slavery to men, see Deissmann, *Licht vom Osten,* Tübingen, 1908, 231-238. Eng.
trans., *Light from the Ancient East,* New York and London, 1910, pp. 322-334.

[55] Paul's use of righteousness in Rom. 6:12 23 is inter
esting. It, rather than God, is put in opposition to Sin,
in verses 13, 16, 18, 19, 20. This fact, taken alone, would
militate against the view that Sin is here conceived of
as personal. But verse 18 shows that righteousness is
used rhetorically for God. The expression, "being freed
from Sin, you became enslaved to righteousness" (v. 18),
becomes in verse 22, "being freed from Sin, but enslaved
to God." This use of righteousness is overlooked by
Kabisch, *Die Eschatologie des Paulus,* Göttingen, 1893,
166.

[56] Despite such utterances as those found in Rom. 1:18-

to Sin, the result will be death. If they choose
to enslave themselves to God, the result will be
eternal life. Sin as a lord pays his servants.[57]
But what a remuneration—Death! Those who
choose to serve God rather than Sin will receive
no pay, for they can earn nothing in his service,
but they will receive from him the free gift of
eternal life.[58]

In its effect upon human experience Sin is
closely connected with the human body. It
reigns in the body.[59] The passions which lead
to transgressions through the law work in our
members, producing fruit unto death.[60] With
the mind one serves the law of God; with the
flesh the law of Sin.[61] The flesh constituted a
weakness in men, rendering the law incapable of
saving them from Sin.[62] Those whose conduct

23, 28; 2:14, Paul nowhere makes perfectly plain how
far salvation was possible in the period preceding the
advent of Christ.

[57] Military lord, probably, in view of the military
weapons, mentioned in Rom. 6:13.

[58] Rom. 6:23.

[59] Rom. 6:12.

[60] Rom. 7:5.

[61] Rom. 7:25. Sin, as a person, is credited with having
a law, just as God is.

[62] Rom. 8:3. This weakness or impotency of the flesh

is determined by the flesh cannot measure up to the righteousness which the law requires.[63] To belong to Christ means the crucifixion of the flesh, with its passions and desires, as the media through which Sin finds expression.[64]

Sin and Death are closely allied in their opposition to men. They entered into human experience at the Fall simultaneously, as cause and effect. "Through one man Sin entered into the world, and, through Sin, Death, and so upon all men Death passed, because all sinned." [65] Death is the logical and inevitable result of Sin.[66] In Death Sin has its triumphant reign.[67] This relation of cause and effect between the cosmic Power Sin, and the natural phenomenon death, has its explanation in the fact that since actual transgressions are the indisputable evidence of

with regard to sin is probably to be understood as a cosmic inferiority to the cosmic power, Sin, rather than as a purely psychic or physiological tendency of the body to commit sin. This verse contrasts the cosmic power of Sin and the cosmic power of Christ, who conquers Sin.

[63] Rom. 8:4-8.
[64] Gal. 5:24.
[65] Rom. 5:12.
[66] Rom. 1:32; 6:16, 21, 23; 7:5, 13.
[67] Rom. 5:21.

allegiance to Sin,[68] God cannot do otherwise than inflict death upon those who are allied with his enemy, Sin. God must ultimately triumph over his cosmic enemies, else there is no hope for the world. All who are allied with these enemies must suffer their fate. Man is not naturally God's enemy, but his creature. It was not intended originally that he should become arrayed against God, but even after that estrangement took place, in the Fall of Adam, God's real purpose for, and disposition toward, man underwent no material change. At no time has he ever desired the death of men. God loves men with a love far surpassing human love. It has been his concern to devise a plan by which he could break the power of Sin over men, and set them free to make another choice between himself and his cosmic enemy. Since the Fall, men have been handicapped by the fact that Sin secured an advantage over them, for which they are not entirely responsible. On the one hand, their allegiance to Sin rendered it impossible for God to do otherwise than reckon them as allies of his adversary. On the other hand, this alle-

[68] Rom. 6:16.

giance, being not originally voluntary on their part, and, indeed, at no time entirely so, it was impossible for men, unaided by a power stronger than Sin, to break the bonds that bound them to their over-lord, Sin, and to present themselves as vassals, or slaves, to God. It was this extremity of men that made necessary God's plan of redemption for them.

Turning now to a consideration of Paul's general view of the nature of the world's redemption, we recall that he regarded it as a two-fold process and that his practical philosophy led him to deal chiefly with the saving of men from Sin and Death, and to allude relatively seldom to the redemption of the cosmos from the evil powers. While it is true that the salvation of men is inseparably connected with the redemption of the cosmos, still the two are, in a way, distinct problems. That Paul in thought differentiated between them becomes evident on examining his vocabulary and his general attitude toward them. When speaking of the redemption of the world, he refers in general terms to the putting down of all rule, authority, power, enemies, and the like.[69]   Or he speaks of the created universe as something which is ultimately at the complete disposal of God. If it now languishes under the sway of demonic powers, this condition was a part of God's purpose for it. Eventually it will realize the purpose which he has had for it from the beginning, namely, the freedom of the glory of the children of God.[70] That the world will be rescued from the sway of the Evil Powers at some point in the near future Paul entertains no doubt. Being inert matter, it has no part to play in its own redemption, of course. With the overthrow of the Evil Powers it passes *ipso facto* under God's beneficent sway.

Paul's representation of the salvation of men is very different from these descriptions of the redemption of the world of matter. In speaking of man's salvation, he uses a great variety of expressions and figures of speech, such as reconciliation, propitiation, righteousness, Passover, and the Mosaic law. These terms are all, however, Jewish in their association, and occur chiefly in those discussions regarding salvation in which

[69] I Cor. 15:24-26.
[70] Rom. 8:20, 21.

Paul encounters opposing views from Judaizing sympathizers. In order to obtain a genuinely Pauline view of salvation, we should select an utterance in which Paul expresses himself untrammeled by any opposing theories, or apologetic purpose. Fortunately we have several such utterances, notably in his first letter to the Thessalonians. From this letter the controversial element is absent. The congregation was a new one. Paul had been driven from their midst by persecution before he had completed his stay. They were beginners in the Christian life. It is not likely that in addressing them he would use language that he had not used when among them. From such a letter we should expect to find the gist of Paul's gospel, as he preached it in Gentile communities, and as he wrote about it when uninfluenced by Jewish traditions and vocabulary. In this letter he recounts briefly the history of the Thessalonian church, dwelling with evident pleasure upon the success of his mission among them and their clear and firm grasp upon the fundamentals of his doctrine of salvation. He says, "We thank God at all times on your account . . . remembering your work of faith, your labor of love, and your steadfastness of hope in our Lord Jesus Christ before our God and Father, knowing, brethren beloved of God, the outstanding features of your conversion, that our gospel was for you, not simply a matter of discourse, but was characterized by power, by the Holy Spirit and by much assurance. . . . For by you the word of the Lord was promulgated widely, not only in Macedonia and Achaia, but in every place your faith in God has gone forth, so that we have no need to say anything. For they themselves announce what sort of access we had to you, and how you turned to God from idols to serve a God living and true, and to await the coming of his Son from the heavens, whom he raised from the dead, namely, Jesus, who rescues us from coming wrath." [71]

It is in the closing sentence of this passage that we have Paul's epitome of his gospel message; in other words, the essentials of the plan of salvation. They are: the worship of the one living and true God, the awaiting of his Son from the heavens, belief in the fact that God raised his Son from the dead, and deliverance

[71] I Thes. I:2-10.

from the coming wrath. These four items may be reduced to one—escape from the coming wrath. The remaining three are subsidiary to this one practical result. The worship of the true and living God is necessary to this deliverance. Neither a dead God nor a false one, such as the Thessalonians had worshiped, could effect deliverance from the impending wrath. The coming of God's Son from the heavens was the time set by God when his wrath would be displayed. The fact that this living and true God had brought his Son back from the region of the dead was the ground of faith, or confidence in God that he could and would deliver men from the wrath which was reserved for his foes, who had held the world in subjection and inflicted unspeakable woes upon men. According to this passage, at least, Paul conceived of salvation as deliverance from the wrath which would be manifested at that eschatological moment when the end would come to "this age," with all its misery and woe, as well as to the Powers of Darkness and Evil which produced this misery and woe, and when the "coming age" of God would be ushered in. This thought is repeated in the following summary: "For God did not appoint us unto wrath, but unto the obtaining of salvation through our Lord Jesus Christ, who died for us, that, whether we wake or sleep (i. e., live until the Parousia takes place or die in advance of it) we may live (thereafter and forever) with him."[72]   Paul's closing wish, or prayer, for the Thessalonians contains the same thought: "May the very God of peace sanctify you wholly, and may your whole spirit and soul and body be preserved blameless until the Parousia of our Lord Jesus Christ.   Faithful is he who calls you, who also will do it."[73]

[72] I Thes. 5: 9, 10.

[73] I Thes. 5:23, 24.   See also 2:19, 20; 4:13-18; 5:1, 2; 2 Thes. 1:5-10; 2:1-12.   It may be objected that it is interpretatively inadmissible to take a more or less isolated representation from this early, simple, and practical letter to the Thessalonians and give to it normative, or standard, value, when it is lacking in those outstanding characteristics of the Pauline soteriology, as we gather them from the so-called soteriological letters, namely, Gal., 1 and 2 Cor., Rom.   We have already intimated that the reason for this difference lies not in Paul, but in the conditions under which he wrote his several letters.   On this point more later.   In the meantime, let it be observed that, if this is the form in which Paul presented the gospel to the Thessalonians on his Second Missionary Journey, he must have presented it in a similar form to the Philippians, Athenians, and Corinthians on this same

The natural interpretation of Paul's utterances on Salvation, as recorded in First Thessalonians, makes evident that man's salvation, when reduced to its lowest terms, means escape from the coming wrath. The same thought is expressed to the Romans in the following passage: "But God commends his own love to us, in that while we were still sinners, Christ died for us. Much more then being reckoned as acceptable (to God) in his blood, we shall be saved from the wrath through him." [74]

It must be borne in mind that this wrath, while now revealed from heaven against all ungodliness and unrighteousness of men who hold down

journey. Moreover, it is difficult to think of his writing as he does to the Thessalonians while he was in Corinth and then of his preaching to the Corinthians a "different gospel." In his letters to the Thessalonians and Corinthians a striking parallel exists. In both letters, Paul testifies to the fact that his preaching was "in power," "in the Holy Spirit," or "in demonstration of the Spirit" (1 Thes. 1:5; 1 Cor. 2:4, 5). But this suggestion will be strengthened as we proceed to a more minute examination of the distinctive features of salvation, as Paul reviewed them for his young converts at Thessalonica. A comparison of the teaching of the other letters on these points will show that the difference between them and the Thessalonian letters is not as great as is sometimes maintained.

[74] Rom. 5:8, 9.

the truth in unrighteousness,[75] is really eschatological.[76] Man's present misfortunes are not an
expression of God's wrath, or displeasure. Man
will suffer punishment and loss in consequence
of his unrighteousness, but this punishment and
loss are not visitations of God's punitive attitude
toward the sinner. They are the natural result
of the workings of the Evil Powers, particularly
Sin and Death. God's wrath is not a vindictive
wrath engendered by the fact that men have
actually committed specific transgressions against
his law. It is cosmic, representing his opposition to the Evil Powers, and will be displayed,
and become operative in the nearly approaching
cosmic catastrophe.[77] The cosmic and eschatological character of God's wrath are set forth in
the following: "But dost thou reckon this, O
man, thou that sittest in judgment on those who
do such things, and yet doest them thyself, that
thou shalt escape the judgment of God? . . .

[75] Rom. 1:18.

[76] I Thes. 1:10; 5:9; Rom. 2:5, 8; 5:9; 9:22-24; 12:19.

[77] Paul actually recommends the turning of the ethical
offender at Corinth over to Satan for the destruction of
the body that the spirit may be saved in the day of the
Lord. (I Cor. 5:5.)

But according to thy hard and impenitent heart treasurest up for thyself wrath in the day of wrath (the day of the Lord) and revelation of the righteous judgment of God, who will render to each one according to his deeds, eternal life [78] to those who by patience in well doing are striving for glory [78] and honor [78] and immortality; [78] but to those who through a factious spirit and disobedience to truth are obedient to unrighteousness, he will render wrath, and indignation, tribulation and anguish upon every soul of man who doeth evil, to the Jew first and also to the Greek." [79]

If man's salvation is fundamentally a rescue from the wrath of God and if that wrath is both eschatological and cosmic, it follows that man's salvation must be also eschatological and cosmic. While for men salvation is an individual blessing, dependent upon their own choice of God rather than of Sin as their master, their salvation is, at the same time, inseparably connected with the redemption of the world from the power

[78] All these are eschatological terms, and are put in opposition to the terms which follow, they being likewise eschatological.

[79] Rom. 2:3-9.

of Satan and his hosts. It is in this sense that man's salvation may be said to be cosmic. This aspect of salvation is expressed in the following words addressed to the Corinthians: "Let no one glory in men. For all things are yours, whether Paul or Apollos or Cephas, or the cosmos or life or Death, or things present or things to come, all things are yours and ye are Christ's and Christ's is God's." [80]

In his letter to the Romans, Chap. 8, Paul most fully sets forth the meaning of salvation. We give herewith a portion of this chapter, paraphrased in harmony with the cosmic interpretation of salvation: "The impending condemnation is removed from those who have committed themselves to the cosmic Christ. For the law of the Spirit, which eventuates in eternal life in Christ Jesus, freed thee from the law of Sin, and of Death. For what law (either the command of God or the Mosaic law) could not do, because flesh, the mark of the human, was weaker than the cosmic power, Sin, against which the law arrayed man, God, by sending his own Son, in the likeness of the flesh of which

[80] I Cor. 3:21-23.

Sin was master, and because of this cosmic power, Sin, overthrew the power of Sin over flesh (i. e., over men) in order that we might have the power to do the things required by the law (i. e., live the ethical life), which power we believers do have, for we now live a life that is not dependent on weak flesh, but on the cosmic power of God, which he dispenses to us through the Spirit." [81]

While in the foregoing passage Paul begins by referring to the eschatological aspects of salvation, he comes later to speak of the effects of salvation in this life. One of these effects, namely, the supremacy over Sin in the ethical life, we discuss later.[82] But before leaving Romans, Chap. 8, we must notice some very important effects of salvation, which are partly experienced in this life and partly in the life to come.

The first of these is that Paul attributes the immortality of believers to the saving work of Christ. He says: "If Christ is in you . . . the spirit is life [immortal] because of righteousness." [83] The effect of Sin and Death upon

[81] Rom. 8:1-4.   [82] See Chapter IV.
[83] Rom. 8:10.

the spirits or souls of men is counteracted. Whereas men's spirits would have perished and thus shared the fate of the cosmic powers, Sin and Death, they are by virtue of the Spirit of God endowed with the principle of eternal life. This effect takes place here and now, in this life. As far as man's spirit is concerned, the redemptive work of Christ restores even here what was lost in the service of Sin and Death.[84] With the bodies of men, however, the case is different. The body dies, i. e., is subject to physical death. As Paul expresses it, "The body is dead because of Sin." [85] At the same time this is only a temporal disability. For Paul the salvation of Christ must be unlimited in its extent by the Cosmic Powers. Even our bodies must be redeemed from the power of Death.[86] And so they are to be, by the same power of God which

[84] Paul seems to entertain the view that the actual participation of the human spirit in the power of God rendered the difference between the present and the future existence of the believer one of degree, not of kind. What made the earthly life undesirable was the excessive burden of the body. The redemption of the body was what called forth sighs and longings (Rom. 8:23).

[85] Rom. 8:10.

[86] All that was lost in Adam must be restored through Christ.

will overthrow all the hostile forces of the universe. The only condition is that we have within us this cosmic dynamic of God. This power
will give life again to our mortal bodies which
have fallen victims to the power of Death, and,
in consequence, have lain in the grave. Our certainty of this is found in the resurrection of
Jesus. "If the Spirit of him that raised up
Jesus from the dead dwells in you, he who
raised Christ Jesus from the dead will make alive
even your mortal bodies through his Spirit that
dwells in you." [87]

There is one more important feature pertaining to salvation, namely, the adoption as sons of
God. If we have the Spirit of God, we have
God himself, for the Spirit is God. To be led
by this Spirit, that is, to be under the sway of
God is to be at one with God in the cosmic
process, particularly in the redemption of the
world and in one's own redemption. God reck-
ons such as his sons and gives them the Spirit,
which reception of the Spirit carries with it sonship, and, in consequence, "we cry Abba

[87] Rom. 8:11. See also Rom. 5:17-21; 1 Cor. 15:20-23;
Phil. 3: 20, 21.

Father." [88]   From sonship Paul advances to the
related idea of inheritance.   The fact that we
are sons renders us heirs of God the Father,
joint-heirs with his Son, Jesus Christ.   This
means that we shall share in all his future glory,
just as we are now sharing in the sufferings
which he endured while on earth.[89]

With this thought, Paul has again got back
to the eschatological aspect of salvation with
which he began Romans, Chap. 8.   In the section embraced in verses 20-25, he focuses his
attention upon the work of redemption, as it
is to affect the created universe of matter, at
the same time never losing sight of the importance which this rehabilitation of the cosmos
has for those who are united with Christ.   In
verses 26-27, he shows how the believers are
kept in perfect accord with God's purposes and
with the entire cosmic process, through the activity of the Spirit in their behalf, especially in
the matter of prayer.   From this vantage point
he contemplates the ultimate goal of the individual's salvation.   This he finds to be conform-

[88] Rom. 8:14-16.   Cf. Gal. 4: 5, 6.
[89] Rom. 8:17-19.

ity to the image of God's Son. This approxima-
tion to the likeness of Christ is for Paul's mind
extremely close, for when we attain to it Christ
becomes the first-born [90] among many brethren.
This means complete identification of the saved
man with God, and all brought about in accordance with God's eternal plan for the redemption
of the world. And we know that for those who
love God all things (all the cosmic forces and
processes) work together advantageously, namely, for those who are called according to his
cosmic purpose. Because whom he foreknew
he also set apart in advance to be conformed
to the image of his Son that the Son might be
the first-born among many who through salvation become assimilated to his likeness and are
therefore his brothers in a cosmic sense.[91]

As far as man's salvation is concerned, Paul's
circuit of thought is complete.[92] He finds man

[90] Rom. 8:29; "The first born only." (Jülicher.)

[91] Rom. 8: 28, 29. See 1 Cor. 15:49; Phil. 3: 20, 21. The
redeemed in glory not only take on the nature of Christ,
but also participate in the exercise of one of his chief
functions, namely, the function of judge at the Great
Day. 1 Cor. 6: 2, 3.

[92] Except for the elaboration of the grounds of assurance on which the believer's hope for this salvation

in the grasp and control of the powers of the underworld, chiefly two of them, namely, Sin and Death. Being human, i. e., flesh, man is inferior in strength and intelligence to these superhuman powers, while, at the same time, his body of flesh constitutes the vehicle, *par excellence,* through which Sin operates for his destruction. For this body has desires and propensities which Sin exploits, and, in so doing, keeps man continually in his service as a slave, inasmuch as these desires and propensities of the body, when thus exploited by Sin, result in a certain group of deeds or actions which are contrary to the nature and purpose of God. Man is helplessly and hopelessly held in this servitude to Satan and his allies, since by his own strength he is incapable of extricating himself from them. To continue in this grasp of the Evil Powers is to suffer eternal destruction. God in his love for man provides a way of escape in a cosmic salvation, which he makes effective through the service and obedience of his Son.

rests. Rom. 8:31-39. Cf. 5:12-21; 6:10-12; 7:24, 25; 8:9-11. The cosmic character of man's salvation is here strongly emphasized.

This salvation not only provides for man's rescue from the thraldom of these cosmic foes, but also provides for a thorough-going rehabilitation and transformation of man in every particular, in spirit, soul and body (flesh). He becomes identified with God in his work for the redemption of the cosmos. This means that he becomes a positive, active force for good and a violent and constitutional foe of every Evil Power and of every manifestation of such Evil Power, particularly in the realm of human conduct. In addition to becoming thus identified with God in this life, he becomes one with him in nature and function in the coming age.

CHAPTER III

In the preceding chapter we have sought to establish the following facts with regard to Paul's teaching on the redemption of the world:

1. Paul had a dualistic philosophy, according to which two opposing cosmic forces, God and Satan, were arrayed against each other in a struggle for the control of the universe.

2. The history of the cosmos was divided into two periods, or ages, "the present age" and the "coming age." During "the present age," Satan and his hosts ruled the world. But "the present age" is reaching its end, and "the coming age" is just about to be ushered in. With "the coming age" the rule of Satan ceases, and the rule of God will be supreme.

3. Man became involved in the cosmic struggle between God and Satan, through his progenitor, Adam, who, because of his disobedience

49

to God, passed under the control of Sin and
Death, carrying along with him his entire progeny, who ever since have suffered countless misfortunes and afflictions in this life and stand
doomed to eternal destruction.

4. God in his love has provided for man a
way of escape from this hopeless condition, and
a complete transformation, in which he attains
to God's own likeness and to a participation in
his functions as ruler and judge of the universe.
This rescue and transformation Paul designates
in several ways, but chiefly by the words salvation (σωτηρία) and redemption (ἀπολύτρωσις).

We have now to inquire how this salvation
was made possible. By what means was it effected? Theology has answered this question by
saying that the means employed was the death
of Christ on the cross, and it has made it to be
its chief task to elaborate this answer and to dis-
cover the philosophy underlying it. In the pur-
suance of this task it has put forward many
hypotheses, out of which have arisen numerous
well-known and widely current theories of the
atonement. Upon a rehearsal or discussion of
these various theories, with their many shades of

difference, we shall not enter, but shall limit ourselves to a division of them into two groups and
a general characterization of the main features
of each group.

Broadly speaking, the theories of the atonement may be divided into two groups, according
to the answer which is given to the question:
Who is affected by the death of Jesus, God or
man? Those theories which claim that the effect of Jesus' death is primarily upon God constitute a group which we may designate the satisfaction group. Those theories which hold that
the effect is primarily upon man constitute a
group which we may designate the ethical group.
In both the satisfaction and the ethical theories
it is assumed that the death of Christ is a sacrifice. The difference between them arises when
the effort is made to determine for whose benefit
the sacrifice is made. Without intending to sit
in judgment on the worth of these theories, we
have cited them for the purpose of bringing to
mind the fact that, while they are far apart in
their answer to the fundamental question,
whether primarily God or man is affected by the
death of Jesus, they are at one as to the fact on

which they predicate salvation, namely, the death of Jesus a sacrifice. This holds, whether the effect be in some way forensic, or juridical, as in the satisfaction theories, or psychic, as in the ethical theories.

The place which theology has assigned to the death of Jesus in the redemptive program having been in this general way determined, it is in order next to ascertain what place it has assigned to the resurrection of Jesus. Usually it has been given a secondary place. Most interpreters of Paul have regarded the resurrection of Jesus as an act in which his death was given divine attestation and approval. The resurrection was needed, so it is said, as an aid to faith, in order to equip the early disciples with the necessary confidence for their mission. To herald salvation as a gift to all men by a Galilean Peasant, who died the shameful death of a malefactor, was a difficult task at best. It was imperative that the missioners be fortified for this undertaking by indisputable proof that the Jesus who died on the cross was really the Son of God. In bringing Christ back from the dead, God the Father set the seal of his approval to the shame-

ful death of his Son, and thereby proclaimed to
the world that the sacrifice which Christ made
on the cross, as an atonement for sin in order to
reconcile God and man, had been accepted by
him and that in the death of Christ the world's
redemption had been effected. In its simplest
outlines this is the significance which is usually
assigned to the resurrection of Jesus.[93]

In favor of this interpretation is to be noted
the fact that it finds support in a comparison of
Paul's utterances regarding the death of Jesus
with those regarding his resurrection, both from
the standpoint of their frequency and of their
relative enthusiastic vehemence. It gains further
support from the fact that the death occupies
the center of interest in at least three of Paul's
principal letters, namely, Galatians, First Corinthians and Romans. While these facts cannot
be contradicted, and while they explain in great

[93] B. Weiss, *Biblical Theology of the New Testament,*
Eng. trans. Edinburgh, 1888, §81 (c) (d). Ger. 1868, 7
Aufl., 1903. Holtzmann, *Lehrbuch der neutestamentlichen
Theologie,* Freiburg und Leipzig, 2 Aufl., 1911, II 121 f.
See additional citations by him. Weinel, *Biblische The-
ologie des Neuen Testaments,* 2 Aufl., Tübingen, 1913, 253.
Jülicher, in J. Weiss, *Die Schriften des Neuen Testaments,*
Göttingen, 2 Aufl., 1908, II 241.

measure the relative preponderance in Christian
theology, from Paul's day to our own, of the
death of Jesus over his resurrection, they nevertheless do not compel the conclusion that this
disparity was present to the mind of the Apostle.
A careful examination of Paul's teaching on the
resurrection of Jesus goes to show that it was
a prime factor in the problem of redemption.
We misinterpret Paul when we represent him
as teaching that salvation was effected by the
death of Jesus apart from his resurrection. The
death and resurrection were not separable, except
for thought. Paul viewed them as two aspects
of one and the same transaction. Together and
only together they constitute the redemptive
work of Jesus. The proof of this is abundant,
as may be seen on comparing the passages cited
below.[94]

The importance of the resurrection is also
shown by the fact that it is referred to apart

[94] I Thes. 4:14; 2 Cor. 5: 14, 15; Rom. 4:23-25; 5:10;
6:8-10; 7: 3, 4; 8:34; 14:9; Col. 1:17-20; Phil. 3: 10, 11.
Feine emphasizes the fact that the death and resurrection
of Jesus should be taken together. However, his interpretation of the resurrection contains nothing distinctive.
Theologie des Neuen Testaments, Leipzig, 2 Aufl., 1911,
298 ff.

from the death of Jesus, not as an attestation of the fact that God has accepted the sacrifice of Jesus' death, as theology has made out, but as an act inseparably connected with those phenomena whereby salvation is made possible.[95] Furthermore, there are certain passages in which the resurrection itself appears to be the determining fact in the redemptive plan. If Christ has not been raised from the dead, then the preaching of the gospel is vain, and believers are yet in their sins.[96] If the death of Jesus alone were the basis of salvation, this could not be true. If, when we were enemies we were reconciled to God through the death of his Son, much more being reconciled, we shall be saved by his life, not his earthly life, but his life-power manifest in the resurrection.[97] In one instance Paul goes so far as to make the resurrection alone the object of faith: "If thou wilt confess with thy mouth Jesus as Lord, and wilt believe in thy heart that God raised him from the dead, thou shalt be saved.[98]

[95] 1 Thes. 1:10; Gal. 1:1; 1 Cor. 6:14; 2 Cor. 4:14; Rom. 1:4; 8:11; Eph. 1:20.
[96] 1 Cor. 15:14, 17. See Rom. 4:24; 6:8-10; 8:34.
[97] Rom. 5:10.   [98] Rom. 10:9.

The importance which Paul attaches to the resurrection as an inseparable part of the redeeming work of Jesus goes to support the dynamic and cosmic view of that work. For, if the resurrection be more than an attestation of the acceptance by God of the sacrifice of his Son, then the resurrection at least has some other than a sacrificial meaning. Apart from the resurrection, the crucifixion of Jesus would have been a triumph for the Rulers of this Age, namely, the Evil Powers of the cosmos.[99]   But in the secret plan of God, devised in his wisdom, which was superior to the wisdom of these Rulers of this Age, Christ came forth victorious from their grasp. Death and the Grave had to surrender him. The resurrection therefore was God's first decisive victory over Satan, from the time when the first man passed under his sway by obeying him rather than God. Since it was by this one act of disobedience on the part of God's first son, Adam, that the many died, so by the act of obedience of this Second Adam the many shall be made to live.[100]   Through this act of obedience Jesus put himself in God's hands, as Adam

[99] I Cor. 2:6-8.   [100] Rom. 5:15.

was at first, and enabled God to make trial of
his strength with Satan.   The fact that Satan
could not hold Jesus in the region of the dead
evinced the cosmic superiority of God over the
Evil Powers.   The resurrection of Jesus is therefore the chief soteriological phenomenon to take
place this side of the Parousia.   Inasmuch as it
marks the initial act in the final overthrow of
Satan, it therefore inaugurates "the coming
age." [101]   It is thus a guaranty of the successful
consummation of the entire program of the redemption of the cosmos.

In approaching a more minute study of Paul's
interpretation of the death of Jesus, we shall lay
aside the presupposition with which most interpreters set out, namely, that in Romans 3:21-26
we have Paul's doctrine of the atonement *par
excellence*.   We are aware that this amounts
almost to a violation of an axiomatic law.   Theology, both exegetical and systematic, is shot
through and through with the assumption that
this classical passage represents distinctly the
Pauline view of the saving significance of the

---

[101] The Christians believed themselves to be already living in the new age, that is, just upon the margin of it.

death of Jesus.[102]   The reasons for holding that
this is not the case will be given later.[103]   For
the present we simply point out the result which
has followed from the assumption above referred
to.   Having decided that the passage in question
sets forth the death of Jesus as a substitutionary,
atoning, sacrificial act, and that this act produces
a psychic effect, of a reconciling character, upon
both God the Father and man the sinner, interpreters have proceeded to supply this meaning to
other utterances of Paul.   They make it apply not
only to those utterances in which the death of
Jesus is simply referred to, leaving the reader
to supply the significance of that act, but also to
those, or at least to some of them, in which it is
evident that the whole framework and setting
is entirely different from that in Romans
3:21-26, passages from which it is impossible,
by any legitimate methods of interpretation, to
extract the theory derived from Romans 3:21-
26, without first importing it into them.

[102] Weinel, *Biblische Theologie des Neuen Testaments,*
2 Aufl., Tübingen, 1913, 254.

Jülicher in J. Weiss: *Die Schriften des Neuen Testaments,* 2 Aufl., Göttingen, 1908, 241.

[103] See pp. 98-109.

It has not been found convenient here to discuss the death of Jesus under the conventional rubrics—Redemption, Reconciliation, Righteousness, Sacrifice, Ransom, Atonement. Some of our reasons will appear in the course of the discussion, but our principal reason had best be given here. Since the days of F. C. Baur, students of Paul have been applying, only little by little, his principle of interpreting the Pauline letters as writings intended to meet particular situations and to answer specific questions which arose in the course of the Apostle's missionary work. The application of this principle has not yet become thorough-going and consistent. This is more true in the constructive field of Biblical theology than it is in the department of exegesis. In the present study, we have made the attempt to be consistent at this point. In his manner of debate, as well as in his manner of life, Paul became all things to all men, if by all means he might gain some. It cannot but lead to confusion to arrange his statements regarding the death of Jesus in a scheme of theology, which represents the conflated ideas of his interpreters from Clement of Rome to Schweitzer. To a degree not duplicated by any other doctrine, the death of Christ was forced into the foreground by the controversies of Paul's day. He handled the question in accordance with the dialectic demands of each community in which it arose. If we are to understand any given utterance of his on the subject, we must take our stand, as nearly as we may, precisely at the point from which he viewed it at that particular moment. Because of the controversial atmosphere in which this particular doctrine was discussed it is more necessary to observe this rule with regard to it than it is with regard to other doctrines, including the resurrection. Endeavoring then to adhere faithfully to this fundamental rule of historical interpretation, we proceed to answer the question with which we set out in this chapter, namely: By what means was salvation effected, or made possible?

If we are correct in defining Paul's view of salvation as a deliverance from the Evil Powers of the cosmos, then we should expect the means by which salvation is effected to correspond with the end to be attained. Does Paul so represent the redemptive work of Christ? Is it cosmic or

sacrificial? It has already been pointed out that
this redemptive work includes both the death and
resurrection of Jesus, but, waiving that point for
the present, let us inquire regarding the death
alone. Did it have to do primarily with meeting
the demands of God's punitive nature, which, it
is claimed by theology, required some expedient
that would allow for the forgiveness of man's
sins? Was the death of Jesus such an expedient? Or was it, according to the ethical theories
of the atonement, primarily a demonstration of
God's love to man, designed to engender a corresponding love in man for God? Or again did
it have to do with the overthrow of the Evil
Powers of the cosmos? How does Paul answer
these questions? That is our problem.

We first consider three passages, taken from
the letter to the Galatians.[104] In the language
of the Revised Version (American Standard
Edition), the first of these passages reads as
follows:

"Grace to you and peace from God the Father,
and our Lord Jesus Christ, who gave himself for

[104] Gal. 1:3-5; 3:13; 4:3-5.

our sins, that he might deliver us out of this present evil world, according to the will of our God and Father: to whom be the glory for ever and ever. Amen."

It is customary to interpret the words, "who gave himself for our sins," as equivalent to, who gave himself up in death on account of our sins, in order to atone for them.[105] Explicitly, the passage does not say this. If this is its meaning, then it is an implied and not an expressed meaning.[106] The passage, taken just as it stands, expresses clearly and definitely the purpose which Jesus had in giving himself for our sins, namely, "that he might deliver us out of this present evil world, according to the will of our God and Father." The words which are here trans-

[105] Sieffert, in Meyer, *Kommentar, Der Galaterbrief,* 9 Aufl., Göttingen, 1899. Lightfoot: "A declaration of the true ground of acceptance with God. The Galatians had practically ignored the atoning death of Christ." *St. Paul's Epistle to the Galatians,* London and Cambridge, 1869.

[106] Zahn recognizes this fact, but assumes that Paul had an atonement for sins in mind, and that his readers would so understand him, because they were accustomed to associate the phrase, "for our sins," which they read in their Greek Bible, with the sin offering. Zahn, *Kommentar, Galaterbrief,* 1905, p. 36 f.

lated "out of this present evil world"
are more accurately translated "out of this
present evil age." It has already been
pointed out that, according to Paul's dualistic philosophy, the history of the cosmos was
divided into "the present age" and "the coming
age," and, furthermore, that this division was
not temporal alone, but moral as well, that is,
indicative of the Powers, or Power, which ruled,
or controlled these two ages respectively. For
this terminology Paul was first of all probably
indebted to post-exilic Judaism.[107] But in the
present instance his use of it was particularly ap-
propriate, since his Hellenistic readers, the Galatians, were strongly of the opinion that "this
world" was ruled by Evil Powers, from which
man needed to be saved. Among these Evil
Powers Paul reckoned the law, at least in the
form in which his Judaizing opponents advocated
it.[108] At the very outset of the controversy,
therefore, Paul declares that Jesus gave himself

[107] Bousset, *Die Religion des Judentums im neutestamentlichen Zeitalter*, 2 Aufl., Berlin, 1906, 278 ff.
[108] For this whole subject see Bousset's excellent discussions, in J. Weiss, *Die Schriften des Neuen Testaments*, 2 Aufl., Göttingen, 1908, II 31 ff., 59 ff.

up for us that he might deliver us from the Evil Powers of this present age.[109]

In this representation the redemptive work of Jesus is regarded as a cosmic phenomenon, an act in the world's drama, in which the power of God is arrayed against the evil spirits, who are holding men in their grasp and subjecting them to all sorts of torture. By some means, not disclosed in this passage, but at any rate in accordance with the will of God, Christ rescues us from these Evil Powers.

The other two passages in Galatians which have been referred to will be considered together. They read as follows:

"Christ redeemed us from the curse of the law, having become a curse for us; for it is written, Cursed is every one that hangeth on a tree." [110]

"So we also, when we were children, were held in bondage under the rudiments of the

[109] Note the emphatic order of the words of the approved reading, "out of the present age (which is) evil." The full meaning is that he might snatch us away from the Evil Powers which control this present age.

[110] Gal. 3:13.

world: but when the fulness of the time came, God sent forth his Son, born of a woman, born under the law, that he might redeem them that were under the law, that we might receive the adoption of sons. And because ye are sons, God sent forth the Spirit of his Son into our hearts, crying, Abba Father. So that thou art no longer a bondservant but a son; and if a son, then an heir through God." [111]

The word here translated "redeem" [112] is the same in both passages. It occurs but two additional times in the New Testament.[113] Wherein consists the redeeming act of Christ? In the first of these passages Christ is said to redeem us from the curse of the law. In the second, he is said to redeem those who are under the law. In the former, the act of redemption is connected, in some way, with his death. In the latter, there is no mention of the death.

[111] Gal. 4:3-7.

[112] ἐξαγοράζω.

[113] Eph. 5:16; Col. 4:5. In both these passages it is used in connection with καιρός, time, or opportunity, and signifies "to make the most of the present allotted time, or opportunity." This usage throws no material light on the passage in hand.

The fact should not be overlooked that the background of Paul's thought in these two passages is very different, although on the surface it does not appear to be so. The entire section, Gal. 3:7–4:7, constitutes an argument in answer to the question which he has raised in 3:1-6, namely, How could you, O Galatians, be so foolish as to exchange a Gospel of faith for one of law? The answer turns on the question of sonship to Abraham, and Paul holds to that throughout the major portion of the passage, including 4:3-7. But 3:10-14 constitutes a parenthesis in the thought, suggested probably by 3:9. The fact that those who are of faith are blessed with the faithful Abraham (vs. 9) suggests the condition of those who are not of faith. They are under a *curse,* a fact which Paul finds supported by the Scripture which says: "Cursed is every one who continueth not in all things that are written in the book of the law to do them." Another Scripture, "Cursed is every one that hangeth on a tree," enables him to prove what he is chiefly interested in here, namely, that the law is not operative in the redemptive scheme. Christ, by hanging on a tree, became a curse.

He redeemed men from a curse. Christ, not the law, is the Redeemer.

It is evident that Paul's logic is defective here. It by no means follows because Christ became subject to a particular curse, namely, the curse pronounced on malefactors who are hanged for the violation of particular provisions of the law, that he thereby brings to an end the operations of the entire law. Even the traditional interpretation of the death of Christ, as the ground for our exemption from the penalty of the violated law, does not fit this case, according to Paul's course of reasoning. We are forced, therefore, to the conclusion that we have here an instance of Paul's use of the rabbinical method of exegesis.[114] He was contending with extreme champions of Judaistic theology, and used their weapons—scripture and rabbinical exegesis.

With vs. 14 the parenthesis closes. Paul resumes his figure of sonship and around it discusses such associated ideas as wills, descendants, inheritance and minority before the law, or legal

[114] For other examples of this type of exegesis, see Gal. 3:16; 4:21-31. Cf. Wrede, *Paulus,* Halle, 1904, 49 f. Eng. trans., *Paul,* London, 1907, 78 f.

infancy.[115]   It is in such a setting, then, that we
find the term *redeem*.   There is no reference to
such ideas as atonement, reconciliation, or forgiveness of sins.   The antithesis which Paul has
worked out at great pains is not that, on the
one hand, of a sinner condemned because of
law; and, on the other hand, of an avenging
God, who must in some way have his sin-punish-
ing nature satisfied in order to overlook the
transgressions of his law.   The antithesis is that
of full legal sonship, on the one hand, and of
legal infancy, or nonage, on the other.   This
legal infancy he further describes in terms of
slavery, affirming that the heir in his nonage
"does not differ from a slave, although he is
lord of all, but is under guardians and stewards
until the day appointed of the father (for his
legal emancipation)." [116]   This statement is
somewhat exaggerated, but because of that very
fact clearly indicates the vehemence with which
Paul would make the important point of his argument.   This point reached, he is able to advance his antithesis from legal sonship versus

[115] Gal. 3:15; 4:3.
[116] Gal. 4: 1, 2.

legal infancy to divine sonship versus slavery.[117]
This is the thought which he really wishes to ar-
rive at and which is so prominent in this letter.

But who are the slaves? Before Christ came
and set men potentially free, all men were slaves.
Since the emancipating work of Christ, those are
still slaves who remain in the condition all were
in before the coming of Christ, i. e., under the
law. Who were the masters, or lords? "The
elements of the cosmos." [118] The "elements"
were personal, spiritual beings, not simple ab-
stractions. They constituted the deities of the
heathen, although "by nature they are not
gods." [119] It was from these false divinities that

[117] Gal. 4:3.

[118] τὰ στοιχεῖα τοῦ κόσμου (Gal. 4:3).

[119] On this interpretation see Everling, *Die paulinische
Angelologie und Dämonologie,* Göttingen, 1888, 66-76.
Also the following literature cited by him, p. 70: Hilgenfeld, *Der Galaterbrief,* 1852, p. 66; *Zeitschr. f. wissensch.
Theologie,* 1858, p. 99, 1860, p. 208, 1866, p. 314. Lipsius,
die paulinische Rechtfertigungslehre, 1853, p. 83. Holsten,
Evangelium des Paulus, I. p. 169. Klöpper, *Der Brief
an die Kolosser,* pp. 360-389. Spitta, *Der zweite Brief des
Petrus und der Brief des Judas,* Halle, 1885 (a. a. O. pp.
265 ff.). See particularly Spitta's quotations from Jewish
literature. See also Deissmann, Art. "Elements," in *Encyclopedia Biblica,* and the literature cited by him. Cf.
Brückner, *Die Entstehung der paulinischen Christologie,*
Strassburg, 1903, 225 ff. Dibelius, *Die Geisterwelt im*

Christ had freed the Galatians. They had, before becoming Christians, been "enslaved" to
them, but, after they came to know God, or
rather to be known by God, it was preposterous
to think of their returning to their former enslavement to deities which were impotent and
contemptible. What has this line of reasoning,
with which Paul concludes this section, to do
with the redemption of men from the law? Our
conclusion is that Paul must have included the
law among these "elements of the cosmos," for
there is no evidence that the Galatians were contemplating in reality a return to their former
idol worship. The only thing in contemplation
was the adoption of the Jewish law as the basis
of salvation. It is this adoption of the Jewish
law as the basis of salvation which Paul charac-
terizes as a return to the enslaving worship of
the "elements." In other words, the law is one
of these "elements," that is, a being, a sentient
existence, an hypostasis, not simply a statute,
prescription, command, or formal requirement.

Glauben des Paulus, Göttingen, 1909, 78 ff. Bousset, in
J. Weiss, *Die Schriften des Neuen Testaments,* Göttingen,
2 Aufl., 1908, 59 f.

Accordingly, when Paul says that Christ redeemed men from the curse of the law, or redeemed those who were under the law, he means to say that Christ liberated them from the control and dominion of a cosmic Power, that was in the same class with those demonic beings, which, as elements of the cosmos, the heathens revered as deities.

Despite the juridical interpretation which theology has given to these two Galatian passages, it appears that, taken as they stand, without our introducing an assumed meaning for them (as Zahn, Sieffert and others do) they set before us the redeeming work of Christ, not forensically, but dynamically. In redeeming men, Christ encountered and overcame the cosmic Powers, which are antagonistic to God and men. The contest was a losing one for men as long as they had to contend with those forces unaided. Christ appeared, sent by the Father, "in the fulness of time," as a Stronger One, and rescued men from the slavery to these Powers, to which slavery they had been appointed until the time set for their acquiring their legal emancipation.[120]

[120] Gal. 4 : 2, 3.

72 PAUL'S DOCTRINE OF REDEMPTION

That Paul gave to the redemptive work of
Christ a dynamic and not a forensic value is
borne out by another fact. In both passages
under consideration Paul expresses the purpose
of Christ's saving work in two different ways.
In the first he says: "Christ redeemed us from
the curse of the law, having become a curse for
us . . . in order that upon the Gentiles might
come the blessing of Abraham in Jesus Christ,
that we might receive the promise of the Spirit
through faith." [121] In the second he says: "But
when the fulness of time came, God sent forth his
Son, born of a woman, born under law, in order
that he might redeem those who are under the law,
that we might receive the adoption as sons." [122]

In both passages the saving work of Christ is
spoken of, first, as a redemption from law, and,
secondly, as an impartation of the Spirit.[123] In
the first expression Paul chooses a terminology
which is suggested by the contention of his

[121] Gal. 3 : 13, 14.

[122] Gal. 4 : 4, 5.

[123] That "the adoption as sons" in Gal. 4:5 is equivalent
to "that we might receive the promise of the Spirit
through faith," in 3:14 is shown by the words following:
"And because ye are sons, God has sent forth the Spirit
of his Son into our hearts, crying 'Abba Father'" (4:6).

Judaizing opponents. In the second expression he uses his own characteristic dynamic terminology. It is in this dynamic terminology rather than the other that he frames the incisive question, with which he introduces this section: "This alone would I learn from you, Received ye the Spirit through works of the law, or through the hearing of faith? . . . He therefore that supplieth to you the Spirit and worketh miracles among you (i. e., probably "by you") doeth he it through the works of the law or through the hearing of faith?[124] It is evident that, while Paul speaks of being redeemed from the law with its curse, his positive and characteristic way of expressing the salvation idea is not in terms of forensic or legal relationship, but of an initial cosmic victory over the Evil Powers by Christ and of an imparting by him to believers of his Spirit, which enables them to assert their supremacy over these Evil Powers and thus to perpetuate the work of Christ.[125]

[124] Gal. 3:2-5.
[125] From the standpoint of Greek thought Paul conceived of these Evil Powers as "the elements of the cosmos." From the standpoint of the Judaizers he regarded the "law" as one of them.

We turn next to an important passage in
First Corinthians. The crucifixion of Jesus occupies a prominent place in the earlier portion of
this letter.[126]   The more important verses are
the following:

"Is Christ divided? Was Paul crucified for
you, or were ye baptized into the name of
Paul?[127] "For Christ sent me not to baptize,
but to announce the gospel, not in wisdom of discourse, lest the cross of Christ be rendered use-
less. For the message of the cross is to them
that are perishing foolishness, but to us who are
saved it is the power of God." [128] "We preach
Christ crucified, to Jews a stumbling block and
to Gentiles foolishness, but to those who are
called, both Jews and Greeks, Christ the power of
God and the wisdom of God." [129] "For I determined not to know anything among you save
Jesus Christ and him crucified." [130]

The discussion of the death of Christ turned,
in Galatians, on the question of method, or
means, not on the question of ultimate fact. The

[126] I Cor. 1: 10–2: 16.
[128] I Cor. 1: 17, 18.
[130] I Cor. 2: 2.

[127] I Cor. 1: 13.
[129] I Cor. 1: 23, 24.

question was not regarding the fact of salvation, but regarding the method of procuring it. The fact of salvation was agreed to by all parties to the controversy. Paul even uses the fact that the Galatians were at the time actually in possession of the Spirit as an argument against the contention of the Judaizers regarding the method of securing salvation. A similar situation is presented in Corinth. There is no dispute over the fact of salvation. The Paul party and the other parties agreed on that point perfectly. The question of difference between them pertained to the method of it.

Similar as these two letters are in this respect, they are equally dissimilar in another respect. In Galatia Paul's controversy had to do with men who maintained that salvation became available through the observance of law. In Corinth his controversy was with men who laid claim to a certain kind of superior knowledge, or wisdom, which obscured the central idea of the gospel, as Paul understood it. In neither case, however, was Paul combating a non-Christian religion. In both instances he was dealing with Christians, and, to use our modern parlance, with certain

theories of Christianity, which were opposed to
his own.   He calls the opposing theory in
Galatia "a different gospel." [131]   The Corinthian
theory he does not characterize as such, and in
fact it was not a "different gospel," in the sense
in which the Galatian heresy was.   It amounted
rather to a misplaced emphasis on philosophical
speculation.

It is important to keep in mind these marked
characteristics of the Galatian and First Corinthian letters.   No actor ever suited the word to
the action or the action to the word more perfectly than Paul suited his figures of speech to
the particular form in which his opponents put
forward their tenets. [132]   In Galatians, he reduced to an absurdity the contention that salvation became available through law, by showing
that Christ, in becoming a curse under the law,
or in being born under the law, rescued men
from the dominion of the demonic Power, Law,
which was one of man's cosmic enemies.   In the

[131] Gal. 1 : 6.
[132] On Paul's skill in dialectic, see Wrede, *Paulus,* Halle,
1904, 7, 24 f.   Eng. trans., *Paul,* London, 1907, 4 f., 35 ff.
On the elasticity of his methods of thought, cf. 48 f. Eng.
trans., p. 77 f.

Corinthian letter, Paul reduces to an absurdity the claims which were made for a superior wisdom by showing that God converted that so-called superior wisdom into foolishness.

Now, the false emphasis on wisdom was found chiefly among a certain group of the members of the Corinthian church, namely, that group which is known as the Apollos party. It was to this group, in particular, that Paul addressed himself in the first three chapters. These partisans of Apollos laid store by two things, the one, that Apollos had baptized them, the other, that, through the possession of a superior knowledge, or wisdom, they had a better interpretation of the gospel than Paul had given them and, by this interpretation, got rid of the offense of the cross. It is with this offense of the cross that we are concerned just now. At bottom, the problem in Corinth was identical with that in Galatia— the offense of the cross.[133]

To us moderns the cross is the most precious of symbols, enshrined in art, made precious by song, immortalized by Paul and glorified by Christ. We share Paul's impatience with the

[133] Gal. 5:11; 6:14.

Galatians and Corinthians in their endeavor to get from beneath its shadow. Under the spell of his rhetoric, we cannot but feel the baseness of the ingratitude and cowardice which prompted so recreant a procedure. But Paul's invective must not spoil our perspective. The simple fact is that the cross constituted an unspeakable burden for the early Christians. They were surrounded by Jews, to whom it was an occasion of offense. It was the storm center, not simply of intellectual controversy, as it appears to us on the written page, but of the actual life of the Christians. It was the chief occasion of the violent persecutions, which in that day came from the side of the Jews.[134]   And, no wonder! The Christians charged that the Jews crucified Christ,[135] and then they held that this crucified Christ was the Savior of the world, thus making salvation dependent on one's committing himself to this Jesus whom the Jews had crucified. With the Greeks the doctrine of a crucified Redeemer encountered all but insuperable difficulties. To

---

[134] I Thes. 2:14-16; Gal. 6:12.
[135] I Thes. 2:15. This persecution existed in Judea, even where the Pauline type of gospel was not preached.

the philosophically inclined it was an absurdity, foolishness.

It is not surprising that, under such circumstances, these early Christian communities, while holding to the fact, and, as they doubtless felt, to the essence of the new religion, were easily attracted to "a different gospel" from that which Paul preached, particularly if it avoided the offense of the cross. It is absolutely necessary to feel the full force of this fact if we are to understand Paul's utterances in the Galatian and Corinthian letters on the subject of the death of Jesus. This subject looms up large in these letters because therein Paul addresses himself to those who, in their endeavor to avoid the persecutions incident to the cross, were perverting the gospel.[136]

Turning now to Paul's method of meeting the arguments of the Apollos party, we find no reference whatever to the law, whereas in Galatians nearly the entire discussion turns on that one point. On the other hand, there is not a single

[136] Paul uses the words *cross* and *crucify* thirteen times in the Galatian and Corinthian letters, five times in all the rest of his letters, not once in Romans.

reference in Galatians to wisdom, or to the wise man, while in the first three chapters of First Corinthians there are more instances of the use of these words than in all the rest of Paul's writings, including the remainder of the Corinthian letters.   Paul first distinguishes between two kinds of wisdom.   The one he calls the wisdom of the world,[137] of men,[138] of this age,[139] of the rulers of this age.[139]   The other he calls the wisdom of God.[140]   However the Apollos party may have characterized their wisdom, Paul classes it with the wisdom of men in contrast with the wisdom of God.   It was not, for all that, an ungodly, irreligious wisdom, as we might imagine from Paul's estimate of it.   It was a method of arriving at God, and of securing the same blessings, which Paul comprehended under his term salvation.[141]

[137] I Cor. I : 20, 21.
[138] I Cor. 2 : 5.
[139] I Cor. 2 : 6.
[140] I Cor. I : 21, 24, 30; 2 : 6, 7.
[141] The statement that the Greeks seek wisdom while the Jews ask a sign (I Cor. I :22) shows that this wisdom belongs to the Hellenistic circle of ideas, not to the Jewish.   Paul's attitude toward Apollos and his party, as compared with his severity toward the Judaizers, in Galatia, indicates that, while he realized the danger of

In opposition to this wisdom as a means of
attaining to salvation, Paul put the heralding of
Christ crucified. In what manner the fact of
Christ's crucifixion effected, or made possible,
salvation he does not indicate. But one thing is
noteworthy, namely, that there is nothing in the
passage to show that the death of Christ was a
sacrifice for sins. Wherein, then, lay its importance? Paul begins his argument by putting the
word of the cross and the foolishness of preaching the crucified Christ in opposition to the wisdom method of obtaining salvation.[142] This was
a contrast between his method of evangelizing
and that of Apollos. There is no attempt on his
part to say how the actual work of salvation is
brought about. That lies with God, both from
Paul's point of view and from the point of view
of Apollos. At the outset, Paul is not concerned
with that question, but he approaches it in 1 :24,
where he shifts his phraseology in such a way as
to bring out the fact that Christ himself, not the
gospel, is the power and wisdom of God. In

the wisdom philosophy of Apollos, he at the same time
distinguished between it and the wisdom of the world.
    [142] 1 Cor. 1 :18, 21-23.

that word *power* we have a clue to Paul's idea. Christ is a dynamic Savior. In so far then as Paul gives any indication whatever of the way in which Christ makes salvation possible for us it is in terms of power, not of sacrifice, atonement or reconciliation.[143]

Is it possible to go further and determine how this power of which Christ was the expression effected salvation? This is the important question. Paul answers it in terms of the particular controversy in hand. This salvation, he affirms, is in accordance with wisdom, not the wisdom in which the Apollos partisans were boasting, but the wisdom of God, a peculiar, mystery wisdom, which is of cosmic significance, as is shown by the fact that it was hidden away secretly by God, who before the ages ordained it for our glory. It was hidden, especially from the cosmic Evil Powers of this age, who, because of their ignorance of this hidden purpose of God in Christ, put him to death. They thought, of course, that they were gaining another victory over God by doing away with his Son, but they

[143] The interpretation of the gospel in terms of power is re-enforced by reference to I Cor. 2:4, 5; 4:20; 5:4.

fell victims to their own devices, and in crucifying the Lord of Glory brought about their own destruction.[144]

By an entirely different route we have reached the same point precisely to which we were led in our study of the death of Christ in Galatians. There it developed that the saving work of Christ is a cosmic, dynamic act. While Christ is said to redeem us from the curse of the law, what is really meant is that he has liberated us from the demonic Powers, or the cosmic Forces of Evil, of which one was the Law. In Corinthians likewise the saving fact in the redemptive work of Christ is a cosmic phenomenon. Christ encountered these demonic Powers, here called "Rulers of this Age." In compassing his death, they seemed to triumph over God. But no, it was only a mock victory.

[144] Cf. Lk. 22:3; Jn. 13:2, 27. See Everling, *Die paulinische Angelologie und Dämonologie,* Göttingen, 1888, 11 ff. Kabisch, *Die Eschatologie des Paulus,* Göttingen, 1893, 177, 182. Wrede, *Paulus,* Halle, 1904, 58 f. Eng. trans., *Paul,* London, 1907, 95 f. Bousset, in J. Weiss, *Die Schriften des Neuen Testaments,* 2 Aufl., Göttingen, 1908. Dibelius, *Die Geisterwelt im Glauben des Paulus,* Göttingen, 1909, 88 ff. For Patristic citations see W. Bauer, *Das Leben Jesu im Zeitalter der neutestamentlichen Apokryphen,* Tübingen, 1909, 522 ff.

Christ, despite his apparent defeat, was the real victor. His death was only one act in the drama. If nothing else had followed he would have been the vanquished one. But something else did follow. There was another act to the drama, and that act demonstrated beyond question that the demons, the Evil Forces of the cosmos, including even the most formidable of them, namely, Death, had been worsted in the contest.

Additional evidence for the cosmic interpretation of the death of Christ is found in 1 Cor. 8:11, which reads as follows: "For on account of your (superior) knowledge the weak one, namely, the brother for whom Christ died, perishes." Rom. 14:15 contains the same thought. Paul was dealing with a practical problem, which arose in consequence of the custom among Christians of eating meat offered to idols, either partaking of it in the idols' temples, as at Corinth, according to the context, or at social gatherings where meat was eaten which had been sold in the markets, after having been offered to idols.[145]   According to 1 Cor.10:19-21, Paul did not regard idols as gods, but he did regard them

[145] 1 Cor. 10:25.

as demons. Hence, he conceived it to be possible
for a believer, while eating meat offered to idols,
to have communion with demons.[146] To do this
was to "perish," for it meant to fall again into
the power of these demons, from which to rescue men "Christ died." The death of Jesus is
therefore thought of, not in terms of reconciliation, or atonement with reference to God, but as
an act of liberation from the demonic Powers.
From this reference it is also to be inferred that
the death of Jesus is efficacious for one's salvation only so long as he continues in dynamic
contact with God, through whose power alone he
is made superior to his superhuman foes.[147]

The eschatological, cosmic and dynamic significance of the redemptive work of Christ is
more fully elaborated in the Ephesian and Colossian epistles than elsewhere in Paul's writings.
This fact was occasioned of course by the strong
Gnostic influence which was at work in the
churches to which these letters were sent. Fundamentally considered, however, the teaching of
these letters regarding the redemption wrought
by Christ does not differ materially from that

[146] I Cor. 10:20.   [147] See Chapter IV.

which we find in the Galatian, Roman and Corinthian letters. While it has been a common
practice to challenge the authenticity of these utterances on the ground of their un-Pauline character, the tendency in this direction grows weaker
as we become better acquainted with Gentile
thought in the days of Paul. In the light of this
fuller orientation, it is an open question as to
whether the thought-forms of Ephesians and Colossians may not have been decidedly more con-
genial to Paul's mind than those found in Rom.
3:21-26.

The principal passages which call for consideration are strikingly similar, and may, for our
purpose, be examined together.[148]   The eschatological character of man's salvation is strongly
brought out in such expressions as: for the praise
of his glory; adoption as sons; sealed in the
gospel of our salvation by the Holy Spirit of
promise, which is a guaranty in this life of the
future redemption; the hope of his calling; the
riches of the glory of his inheritance in the saints.
In Colossians, the eschatological aspect of salvation is expressed when it is said to procure a

[148] Eph. 1:3-23; Col. 1:3-23.

portion of the lot of the saints in light, and to rescue us out of the power of darkness (pertaining to this life) and to transport us into the kingdom of the Son of his love.

The dynamic and cosmic character of salvation is indicated in the following expressions, taken from the Ephesian passage: "the one who works in all things;" [149] "the exceeding greatness of his power to us who believe according to the inworking of the might of his power, which he wrought in Christ, when he raised him from the dead, and made him to sit at his right hand, etc." [150] The form in which this power was manifested is also indicated, namely, in the raising of Christ from the dead and in the seating of him at the right hand in the heavens, far above the hosts of intermediary beings, such as the Rulers, Authorities, Powers and Lordships. Along with these demonstrations of that cosmic power which was operative in Christ goes the putting of all enemies under his feet and the elevation of Christ to the headship of all things.[151]

[149] Eph. 1:11.   [150] Eph. 1: 19, 20.
[151] Eph. 1:20-23.

In Colossians the dynamic aspect of salvation is similarly expressed.[152] The statement that Christ snatched us from the Power of Darkness and transported us into the kingdom of the Son of his love is strikingly dramatic. The more distinctively cosmic significance of Christ himself is brought out in the section following.[153]

It is worthy of notice that Paul maintains almost a uniform silence regarding the actual process by which the saving work of Christ was accomplished. This is the case, whether one view that work dynamically or sacrificially. Theology has never been able to tell just why or how the death of Christ could and did effect a reconciliation with God. Theories have been advanced to explain it, but these theories have been drawn largely from analogies in human affairs, whether judicial, governmental or parental. They have been imported into the Pauline theology, and not drawn from it. Likewise, if one examines those passages in which the cosmic and dynamic character of the redemptive work of Jesus is indicated, he will find as a rule, statements of fact, not of method of procedure, or of

[152] Col. 1:11-13.   [153] Col. 1:15-23.

philosophy. How the death and resurrection of Jesus accomplished for men a rescue from the Evil Powers is usually left undisclosed.

This striking fact may, in part at least, be accounted for by Paul's use of the word *mystery*. When using this word, he seems to have in mind the real content, or gist of the gospel, as in the words, "Christ in you the hope of glory," [154] or in the following summary of the outstanding facts of the gospel, which taken together are denominated "the mystery of righteousness." These outstanding facts are that Christ was:

"Manifest in the flesh,
Justified in (the) Spirit,
Seen of angels.
Preached among the nations
Believed on in the world
Received up into glory." [155]

To this rule of silence touching the actual process by which redemption was accomplished, there seems to be one exception, a passage which

[154] Col. 1 : 26, 27.
[155] 1 Tim. 3 :16. The fact that this passage is found in one of the Pastoral Epistles has no special significance here, since each of the items here enumerated can be duplicated in the acknowledged group of letters, as constituting the momenta of the soteriological career of Jesus.

reads, in the Revised Version, as follows:
"Having despoiled (Margin: having put off from
himself) the principalities and the powers, he
made a show of them openly, triumphing over
them in it." [156]   It is not improbable that we have

[156] Col. 2:15. Bousset, in his article on Gnosticism
(Encyclopedia Britannica, Ed. 11, p. 154), has an interesting suggestion regarding this difficult passage: "In
the Manichaean system it is related how the helper of
the Primal Man, the spirit of life, captured the evil
archontes, and fastened them to the firmament, or according to another account, flayed them, and formed the
firmament from their skin (F. C. Baur, *Das manichäische
Religionssystem,* Tübingen, 1831, 65), and this conception
is closely related to the other, though in this tradition
the number (seven) of the *archontes* is lost. Similarly,
the last book of the *Pistis Sophia* contains the myth of
the capture of the rebellious *archontes,* whose leaders
here appear as five in number (Schmidt, *Koptisch-gnostische Schriften,* p. 234, seq.)." Here is attached the following foot-note: "These ideas may possibly be traced
still further back, and perhaps even underlie St. Paul's
exposition in Col. 2:15." Bousset made the same suggestion, and with similar caution, in his *Hauptprobleme der
Gnosis,* Göttingen, 1907, 54. The Gnostic citations which
he gives seem not to have influenced his translation
of ἀπεκδυσάμενος, which has given interpreters much
trouble. He supplies *Christus* as subject, and trans-
lates: "Christ drew off their military equipment from
the Mighty Ones and the Powers" (*Christus den
Mächten ihre Rustung abgezogen*). May not ἀπεκδύομαι
mean *to flay?* This meaning is not remote from Col.
3:9." The appropriateness of the use of the substantive
in Col. 2:11 is noted, though not precisely in this sense,

here a ray of light thrown on the occult passage,
"seen of angels." [157]

There are several passages in the Corinthian
letters which call for consideration because of
the fact that, at first glance, they seem to indicate an atoning value attaching to the death of
Christ. The first of these reads as follows:

by Abbott, *International Critical Commentary on Ephesians and Colossians,* New York, 1897. The following
(quoted by Dibelius, p. 138) is suggestive. Hades inter-
rogates Satan: δι' ποίαν ἀνάγκην ᾠκονομήσας σταυρωθῆναι τὸν
βασιλέα τῆς δόξης εἰς τὸ ἐλθεῖν ὧδε καὶ ἐκδῦσαι ἡμᾶς; "Through
what sort of necessity did you come to crucify the King
of Glory and thereby to bring him here to strip (or flay)
us?" *Act. Pil.* XXIII. (Discens. VII.). That ἐκδύω with
δέρμα means to flay is shown by the following: Μαρσύας
τὸ δέρμα ἐκδύεται "Marsyas is flayed." Palaeph. 48. 3. It is not
intended to suggest that the verb as Paul uses it means
literally to flay, but that its use here is due to this primitive notion which Bousset believes to underlie the passage.
We should supply neither the word skin nor *military
equipment,* but should abstract the notion and translate:
deprived of their power.

After I had written the foregoing note, my attention
was called to the following translation of Col. 2:15 by
Nairne: "Having stripped off the garment of authorities
and powers which seemed His right, He publicly flouted
such shows of divinity after having led them captives in
His truly triumphal progress to the cross." Nairne, *The
Epistle of Priesthood,* Edinburgh, 1913, p. 67 note. The
point of chief interest is the translation of ἀπεκδυσάμενος
by the phrase, "having stripped off the garment."

[157] 1 Tim. 3:16.

"For our Passover has been sacrificed even
Christ." [158] On the surface, this looks like a
direct and explicit statement of the fact that the
death of Christ was regarded by Paul as a sacrifice for sins, effecting a propitiation of God in
our behalf. If this thought was present to the
Apostle's mind, it receives no emphasis in the
passage. The context is pronouncedly ethical not
theological.[159] Paul was handling a case of gross
immorality. He was surprised and disappointed
that the Corinthians, instead of being humiliated
over gross sin in their midst, were puffed up.
They should have ejected the offending person
from their midst at once. According to Paul's
conception, the life of the individual Christian
should be free from sin. Likewise, the Corinthian community, that is, the local church,
should be actually and literally free from sinful
members. The presence of this flagrant and un-
repenting sinner in the Corinthian church
brought before his mind the picture of leaven
in a mass of meal. A small quantity affects an
entire mass. From this he easily passed to the
Jewish custom of clearing the house of all leaven

[158] I Cor. 5:7.   [159] I Cor. 5:1-8.

before the beginning of the Passover. Regarding the ethical offender still as this leaven, which should be exterminated from the house, he exhorts the Corinthians to get rid of him, in order that they may become a new lump of meal, "just as you are," hypothetically, "leavenless," that is, free from sin and sinners. The statement in question is at this point abruptly thrown in and is followed by one which shows that it did not divert the Apostle's interest from the ethical to the theological. Together they read as follows: "For our Passover, Christ, has been sacrificed; wherefore let us keep the feast, not with old leaven, neither with the leaven of malice and wickedness, but with the unleavened bread of sincerity and truth."

Everything goes to show that it was the season, or time of the Passover, rather than the slain lamb, the victim of the Passover, which was important.[160] It was the season of the feast, not the victim, which called for the house-cleaning. Paul pictured the supposedly brief period of time

[160] τὸ πάσχα (the paschal sacrifice) frequently means the season of the passover. Mt. 26:2; Mk. 14:1; Lk. 2:41; 22:1; Jn. 2:13, 23; 6:4; 11:55; 12:1; 13:1; 18:39; 19:14; Acts 12:4; Heb. 11:28.

in which they were then living, namely, the period between the death of Christ and his Parousia, as a kind of Paschal-feast time. As such, it was a time in which the house, that is, the local Christian community, should be absolutely and literally free from leaven, in this case, the ethical offender.[161]

But even if one is disposed to press the analogy between the dying Christ and the Paschal lamb, he will find it difficult to extract from it the idea of propitiation. Originally the paschal lamb was slain, not for the purpose of averting God's anger, or wrath, but for the purpose of marking the homes of the Israelites in such a way as to divert the destroying angel. The expedient was devised by God in his love for his people, and was thereafter celebrated as a memorial, not of God's propitiation, but of the great deliverance which he wrought for his people.

In 1 Cor. 6:20 and 7:23 there occurs the expression, "You were bought with a price." In both passages the important consideration is the

---

[161] The last word on the subject shows that the important thing was to get rid of the offender: "Cast out the evil one from among you" (1 Cor. 5:13), perhaps with Deut. 24:7 in mind.

fact of God's proprietorship in the Christian, not the process of purchase. In the first instance, Paul reminds the Corinthians that they are not at liberty to do what they please with their bodies, since their bodies are God's temples, their owners being his property by right of purchase. In the second instance, Paul is pointing out, rather after the manner of the Stoic philosophy of his day, the fact that it is a matter of indifference whether one be a slave or a freeman, provided he be a believer, for in that case he is a freeman, although he is a slave of God, since he belongs to God by purchase.

In both cases Paul seems to be using a figure drawn from the common custom of freeing slaves through their fictitious purchase by a deity, at whose temple the transaction took place.[162] As is frequently the case with Paul's analogies, so with this one there is wanting a complete correspondence between the custom of his time and the point he is making. In 1 Cor. 6 : 19, 20 he blends the notion of temple with that of slavery. The bodies of believers belong to God as his temples. Almost as an afterthought

[162] See p. 28, Note 54.

is thrown in the fact that the owners of these bodies are bought with a price, whether as slaves or as buildings is not stated. In 1 Cor. 7:23 the figure is much more fitting. The ransom price is paid by God, whose slaves the ransomed become.

In neither case does Paul tell what the ransom price was, but he presumably thought of it as the death of Christ.[103] Nor does he state who the former lord, or owner, of the ransomed one was, to whom, according to the custom, the ransom price was paid. These passages throw no light on this question, except that the price was not paid to God, as certain interpretations of the atonement have required. This fact is clearly brought out in 1 Cor. 6:19, 20, where God is represented to be the purchaser.

There remains still for examination the important passage in Rom. 3:21-26, and two besides, which will be considered in connection with it. We have already noted the fact that the passage in Romans is the one most of all to which theology has gone for its understanding of Paul's interpretation of the death of Jesus.

[103] Cf. 1 Pet. 1:18, 19; Rev. 5:9.

The result has been a sacrificial and propitiatory view of redemption, rather than a dynamic and cosmic view of it.

The crux of the problem which this passage presents is thus succinctly stated by Sanday: "It is impossible to get rid from this passage of the double idea (1) of a sacrifice; (2) of a sacrifice which is propitiatory. . . . And further, when we ask, Who is propitiated? the answer can only be 'God.' " [164] With minor changes, here and there, this interpretation may be taken as typical of that of the majority of scholars.[165] It is important to indicate the leading ideas on which it is based and to determine whether or not these ideas may be thoroughly established from the remainder of the Pauline literature.

In the main, it rests on five presuppositions:

1. That propitiation or propitiatory ($\grave{\iota}\lambda\alpha\sigma\tau\acute{\eta}\rho\iota\text{ov}$) can refer here only to God. Whether the

---

[164] *International Critical Commentary on the Epistle to the Romans,* New York, 1895, p. 91.

[165] B. Weiss, in Meyer, *Kommentar, Der Brief an die Römer,* 9 Aufl., Göttingen, 1899. Zahn, *Kommentar, Römerbrief,* Leipzig, 1910. Lipsius, in Holtzmann, *Hand-Commentar zum Neuen Testament,* Freiburg, 1892. Jülicher, in J. Weiss, *Die Schriften des Neuen Testaments,* 2 Aufl., Göttingen, 1908.

context requires this reference or not is open to
question. That the word itself requires it seems
not to have been proved.[166]

2. The use of the word righteousness (δικαιοσύνη) taken in connection with God, according to which he is compelled to punish all
transgressions against his law.[167] Now, if this
word has this meaning here, the usage has no
parallel elsewhere in Paul, unless it be in Rom.
3:5, which itself is doubtful. Everywhere, aside
from these three instances in question,[168] it has
an entirely different meaning, we might almost
say an exactly opposite meaning, according to
which, instead of being an attribute of God, it is
a state, or condition of man.[169] Instead of its

[166] According to Deissmann, it may refer either to God or
to men, *Zeitschrift für die neutestamentliche Wissenschaft,* 4 (1903) p. 193. Regarding its meaning he has
the following to say: It "signifies 'the propitiatory thing,'
'the means of propitiation.' What the propitiatory thing
that is actually intended may be has to be determined in
each case by the context." Art. Mercy Seat in *Encyclopedia Biblica,* 1902.

[167] Zahn, *Kommentar, Der Römerbrief,* 1 und 2 Aufl.,
Leipzig, 1910, 192, 196.

[168] Rom. 3:5, 25, 26. B. Weiss, in Meyer, *Der Brief an
die Römer,* 9 Aufl., Göttingen, 1899.

[169] Deissmann holds that throughout this passage the
word has only this meaning. *Zeitschrift für die neutes-*

representing an inherent necessity laid upon God to punish sin, it signifies the sinner's acceptance with God and the assurance of immunity from punishment for his sins.[170] That two such antagonistic meanings should attach to the same word, and in the same context, without some explanatory statement, is hardly probable.

3. The use of the word just ($\delta i \kappa a \iota o s$) in the sense of hostility to sin, by which an antithesis is established between it and the cognate verb following. Accordingly the thought runs: In order that he might evince his hostility to sin and yet accept, without punishing, the man who exercises faith in Jesus.[171] This meaning for $\delta i \kappa a \iota o s$ is not discoverable elsewhere in Paul's letters. It is uniformly used in a good, favorable and kindly sense.

4. God is represented as sacrificing Jesus in order to propitiate himself. We may well be-

tamentliche Wissenschaft, 4 (1903) p. 211. Jülicher adopts this meaning in verse 26, leaving, according to him, only two exceptions to the uniform meaning, namely, Rom. 3:5, 25. J. Weiss, Die Schriften des Neuen Testaments, 2 Aufl., Göttingen, 1908.

[170] Rom. 1:17; 3:21, 22; 10:3; Phil. 3:9.

[171] Rom. 3:26. Sanday's effort to relieve his interpretation of this antithesis does not appear to be successful.

lieve that this paradox would have been as difficult of explanation for the Christians of the first century, whether Jews or Greeks, as it is for those of the twentieth. We can afford to raise the question whether or not such a representation can be consistently held to without its being clearly vouched for by other utterances of Paul.

5. The nature of God is such that he can forgive sins, provided he metes out punishment to someone, but he cannot forgive sins if punishment is not inflicted on someone. This thought, which is the foundation of the usual interpretations of this passage, as well as of the propitiatory theories of the death of Jesus, does violence to our notions of God, and ascribes to him a moral standard far below what Jesus required of men.[172] If it be said that it is distinctly a Pauline teaching, and in some way to be explained on the basis of his rabbinic training, this explanation must account for two facts: first, such an idea finds nowhere

---

[172] Mt. 6:12-15; 18:21-35. Is the difficulty diminished or increased by the fact that the victim was himself innocent and therefore not deserving of the punishment?

else explicit expression in the utterances of Paul;
and, secondly, the bulk of Paul's teachings on
the attitude of God to the sinner shows that attitude to be one of love, far surpassing human
love.[173]

If we approach this passage untrammeled by
the interpretation which is usually given it, we
observe at the outset that the theme of Romans
is not that God has provided salvation through
the propitiatory death of Jesus. As first announced, it is as follows:

"For I am not ashamed of the gospel: for it is
the power of God unto salvation to every one
that believeth; to the Jew first, and also to the
Greek. For therein is revealed a righteousness
of God from faith unto faith, as it is written,
But the righteous shall live by faith."[174]

The salient points in this statement are that
the gospel is the power of God at work for salvation through faith on the part of those who
accept it, whether they be Jews or Greeks. The

---

[173] On the difficulties presented to our thought by the
customary interpretation of this passage, see Sanday, op.
cit. pp. 93 f. and Jülicher in J. Weiss, *Die Schriften des
Neuen Testaments*, 2 Aufl., Göttingen, 1908, II. 242.

[174] Rom. 1:16, 17.

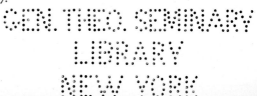

gospel is regarded from the dynamic, not from the sacrificial point of view, that is, if we take the words just as they stand. Analyzing the material lying between these verses and 3 : 21-26, we find that it constitutes a long parenthesis, and that 3 : 21-26 amounts to a resumption or restatement of the theme as found in 1 : 16, 17.[175]

Now if the words *righteousness* and *just* be given their ordinary sense according to Paul's usage, and if *propitiatory* be referred to men and not to God, we have a meaning in these words

[175] In Rom. 1 :18–3 :20 Paul proves that all men, Jews as well as Gentiles, need salvation from the impending doom. But this long argument has removed the theme of the epistle to a great distance. Hence he states it afresh (3 :21-26). In 3 : 21, 22a there is no essential addition to 1 : 16, 17. In 3 : 22b, 23 there is an epitome of 1 :18– 3 :20, that is, the necessity for salvation on the part of all, Jews and Gentiles. In 3 :24-26 there is an answer to the question as to how the salvation referred to has been made and is available for men. This availability rests upon faith in Christ, who by his redemptive act, has effected salvation. Verses 27-31 of Chap. 3 answer objections and expand the thought, "to the Jew first and also to the Greek" (1 :16b). With Chap. 4, the argument proceeds in line with the problem of the letter, namely, the denying of the claim of the Jew that Judaism presented to men the true and only way of salvation. The absence of the word δύναμις does not eliminate the idea of power, for that notion is involved in faith, which Paul regards dynamically, not intellectually.

throughout consistent with Paul's thought. It
runs as follows: God set forth Christ as an act
for the propitiation of men through faith in his
blood for the purpose of showing God's willing-
ness, in his forbearance, to accept men as righteous, despite the sins of the past, for the purpose
of showing this plan of acceptance, which he has
brought forth at this present time in order to
show himself to be fair and good and therefore
ready to receive the man who puts his faith in
Christ.

It may be objected that this interpretation
gives to the death of Christ purely an ethical significance. This would be the case, no doubt, if
this were Paul's only word on the subject, or if
all his other utterances were framed on this
model. But neither of these alternatives corresponds with the facts. We believe that it has
been clearly shown in our study that Paul, in numerous instances, spoke of the death of Jesus as
a cosmic and dynamic fact, which, along with
his resurrection, effected a deliverance of mankind from the control of the Evil Powers of the
cosmos. The significant thing about the representation in Rom. 3: 21-26, is that it is highly

dramatic and that the purpose of the dramatic presentation is to make clear to men, to show forth to them, God's righteousness, whether righteousness be regarded as an attribute of God or as a God-provided state of acceptance with himself assured to men in Christ. The important point is that Paul conceives the death of Christ as producing a dramatic effect upon the minds of men, whether we interpret the ultimate effect of that death as a propitiation of God, or as an overcoming of the demonic Powers.

If this is so, we have in Rom. 3: 21-26, not Paul's primary or fundamental conception of the death of Jesus, but a secondary, or homiletical conception of it. Aside from the part which it played in the actual accomplishment of salvation, it had a subsidiary result in the effect which it produced on the minds of men in their attitude to God. It served to reconcile men to God. Such reconciliation was necessary, because men, under the dominion of Sin, had committed many actual transgressions. These transgressions constituted them the slaves and allies of God's enemy, Sin. God could not count them as his sons, the heirs of his blessedness, so long as they con-

tinued their alliance with his foe. This alliance
had to be broken and a new one formed. Men
had to muster in as God's forces, array themselves against the demonic Powers, and become
positive in their attitude towards the good. But
because of their alliance with God's cosmic enemies, men knew that his wrath must be visited
on them. It had been revealed from heaven.[176]
In the eschatological catastrophe they would
share a fate similar to that which awaited the
demonic Powers, to whom they owed allegiance.
There was no hope for men in this condition.
By their own acts they had constituted themselves the enemies of God, and there was nothing to do but wait for his judgment. They had
no reason to think that God would be willing
to regard them in any other light than that of
enemies. But the death of Christ demonstrated
this view to be erroneous. For the death of
Christ was an expression, not only of God's love
for men in general, but of God's love for men
who are hostile to him.[177] This demonstration
of God's love was a guaranty of the fact that it
was possible for men to shift their allegiance

[176] Rom. 1:18.   [177] Rom. 5:7, 8.

from Satan to God.   It constituted therefore the basis of reconciliation.

As we have said, the idea of reconciliation was not primary in the death of Christ.   It was incidental.   As far as men were concerned it was necessary, but this necessity lay entirely in men. There was nothing whatever from the side of God that required it.   Despite the absence from the Pauline writings of any statement to the effect that it was necessary from God's side, interpreters have predicated a necessity arising out of the nature of the case, so to speak.   The very notion of reconciliation, we are told, requires an effect to be produced upon both parties to the reconciliation.   This theory presupposes a sacrificial significance to attach to the death of Christ, and recognizes but three parties to the transaction—God the injured one, Man the offender, Christ the victim.   If the demonic Powers be introduced as a fourth factor into the problem, Christ becomes a deliverer, who, in man's behalf, enters the field against them. Can he be at the same time a victim sacrificed to God?   The two ideas seem to be mutually exclusive.   If Christ was a sacrifice reconciling

God, then it is inconceivable that he should also
be a cosmic Redeemer vanquishing God's enemies, the Evil Powers.

In contemplating the death of Christ, Paul
does not think of God as a deity whose wrath
must be appeased nor as a judge who must be
provided with some extraordinary expedient, by
which he may not be too lenient regarding the
past violations of his law, and yet at the same
time forgive transgressions of that law. Paul
regards God rather as a helper, a champion of
those who are engaged in an unequal contest,
namely, men of flesh and blood contending with
an adversary, or rather innumerable adversaries,
of a higher order of being, and consequently
superior to men both in intellect and power.
Christ, God's representative, his chosen champion, goes to the rescue of men. He goes in
love and sympathy. The secret plan devised by
God for overthrowing these stronger foes was
the death of Christ.[178] This therefore was
primary. The death of Christ had its necessity
not in men, not in men's sins, not in God, but in
the wisdom of God as he confronted the task

[178] I Cor. 2:7-10.

of rescuing men from the sovereignty of Satan, under whose power Adam's disobedience had placed them.

To put his Son at the mercy of the demonic Powers and to permit them to put him to death by the shameful means of the cross was an act of supreme love on the part of God. As indisputable evidence of that love, it assures men that, if they desire to transfer their allegiance from these Powers of evil to God and thereby become sharers in the victory he has wrought over these Powers, there will be no barrier to their doing so, in so far as God is concerned.

In the foregoing interpretation of this classical passage, all the factors in the redemptive problem are harmoniously related. There is no conflict between God's wrath and his love, or between his justice and his mercy. His love for man is uniform and his wrath against the Evil Powers is uniform. His wrath against man's transgressions is secondary. It is a consequence of man's alliance with these Powers. God the Father did not punish an innocent sacrificial victim in permitting his Son to die for men, for his death was not a sacrifice propitiating God, but a cosmic encounter. Christ alone could perform this work, because man, in the weakness of sinful flesh, was unable to cope with superhuman adversaries. The death of Jesus was therefore vicarious, but its vicarious character was due, not to the fact that God put him to death instead of us, but because only by his death and resurrection could he vanquish our enemies and set us free, and thus make it possible for us to live eternally with God.

The two passages that, as we have said, should be considered in connection with Rom. 3:21-26, and in the light of the interpretation which we have given to it, are: Gal. 2:15-21 and 2 Cor. 5:11-6:2. The Galatian passage deals with the question of righteousness; the Corinthian passage, with the question of reconciliation.

The Galatian passage contains Paul's argument against Peter at Antioch. Over the fact that men attained unto righteousness, or acceptance before God, there was no dispute. The only point of difference between Paul and the Judaizers was as to the means or method by which righteousness was attained to, the alternatives being faith in Christ, or works of the law.

Verses 15-18 contain little more than a repeated asseveration of Paul's contention that righteousness was through faith in Christ. The question as to how righteousness, or salvation, is made a possibility in the economy of God is not touched. The discussion is practical, not philosophical. In vss. 19-21, a different idea from that of righteousness is introduced, namely, that of dying to the law, which is equivalent to dying to Sin, and living to God. This is accomplished, on the one side, by being crucified with Christ, and on the other by being mystically united with Christ, and therefore a partaker of his life-giving power, which, as is shown later, gives to the believer superiority over his cosmic foes. Nowhere does the passage contain an allusion to the death of Christ as a sacrifice which serves to propitiate God.

There is nothing in this passage which requires a modification of the interpretation which we have given to Rom. 3:21-26. On the contrary, it serves to strengthen it, particularly with respect to the secondary, or homiletic character, which it assigns to the passage. This Galatian passage shows the same dialectic peculiarities

which we have noted in the case of other passages.[179]   Here, as in the other instances, Paul
begins by using the terminology which the question at issue required, namely, righteousness
through faith in Christ.   Having reduced the
contention of his opponents to an absurdity, he
sets forth the facts of salvation in his own
favorite terminology, that of power and life.
Without pressing this point unduly, we believe
that the dialectic principle, here referred to, is
followed in Romans also, only on a broader scale.
Aside from the thesis laid down in Rom. 1 :16,
which defines the gospel in terms of power, the
first part of the discussion, that is, from Rom.
1 :17 through Chap. 7, is carried on largely in
the terminology of Judaism, leading terms being
righteousness, law, works, Abrahamic sonship,
and the like.   But with Chap. 8 Paul abandons this
terminology and expresses himself in what we
believe to have been his favorite nomenclature,
power, life, freedom, glory, and in terms connot-
ing superiority over the intermediary beings.[180]

Turning to the Corinthian passage (2 Cor.

[179] Pp. 72 f.
[180] See especially Rom. 8: 2, 6, 10-14, 35-39.

5 : 11–6 : 2), we find a strong utterance on the
reconciling effect of Christ's death in the following: "And all things are of God, who reconciled
us to himself through Christ and gave to us the
ministry of reconciliation, to wit, that God was
in Christ reconciling the world unto himself, not
reckoning their trespasses against them, and giving to us the word, or message, of reconciliation." [181]

We have here another excellent example of
that striking characteristic of Paul's thinking to
which reference has just been made.   Paul is
viewing the central fact of the gospel, the redemptive work of Jesus, not from the standpoint
of its philosophic explanation, but from the
standpoint of his special dialectic need at this particular time.   His problem differs from what it
was in Galatians, First Corinthians and Romans.
In each of these letters, while the personal interest was more or less present, questions of a theological character were thrust into the midst of
the debate.   In Second Corinthians, on the other
hand, Paul is concerned with personal complaints
which have been lodged against him, one of these

[181] 2 Cor. 5: 18, 19.

being, as it seems, a suggestion that he is men-
tally unbalanced. Paul sees the personal affec-
tion and devotion of his spiritual children wan-
ing, and he seeks to reinstate himself in their
favor. He must win the estranged Corinthians.
They must be *reconciled* to him. This gives him
his key—*reconciliation*. Seizing upon this aspect
of the death of Jesus, he uses it with consum-
mate skill to his present purpose. He reminds
his readers that he must in no sense be regarded
as one acting in his personal capacity or for his
personal benefit. He is an ambassador of God.
His message is one of reconciliation. He says:
"On behalf of Christ, therefore, we are am-
bassadors, as though God were entreating at our
hands: we beseech you, on behalf of Christ, be
ye reconciled to God." [182] He all but identifies
himself with Christ in his pleading with them to
be reconciled to God. The dilemma in which this
placed the Corinthians is evident. Their refusal
to be reconciled to Paul, as God's ambassador,
would amount substantially to a refusal to be
reconciled to his principal, God. This would be
equivalent to a rejection of Christ, whose re-

[182] 2 Cor. 5 :20.

demptive work was the substance of the reconciling message, which God was sending by his ambassador, Paul.[183]

Like the Galatian passage, just considered, this one suggests no modification of the results arrived at in the study of Rom. 3:21-26. It furnishes additional evidence in support of our conclusion that Paul did, at times, regard the death of Christ from a homiletic, or practical, standpoint. When so doing, he conceived of its having a reconciling effect on men, because it was an expression of God's love for them, in that he permitted his Son to die in their behalf. In this sense and to this extent the death of Jesus has an ethical significance.

We have concluded our study of the means, or method, by which God made possible the salvation of men. The method of effecting salvation corresponded with the nature of salvation. Salvation being cosmic, the method of its accomplishment was cosmic. This method was devised in the beginning, and was wrought out in the unrevealed wisdom of God. It consisted in permitting his Son to be put to death by his cosmic

[183] Observe that "us" (2 Cor. 5:18), refers to Paul.

foes, the demonic Powers, afterward to be rescued from their control by the superior power of
God in the bringing back of his Son from among
the dead. This cosmic triumph had special reference to Sin and Death, and was chiefly in behalf
of men, for thereby the absolute dominion over
men by these Powers was brought to an end.
Man thus liberated was placed in position to ap-
propriate the superior cosmic power of God for
his salvation. There was also a secondary effect attaching to the death of Jesus. As an un-
paralleled and unreserved demonstration of
God's love for men, it served to lead men to repentance and to the service of God and in consequence to salvation.

CHAPTER IV

THE COSMIC POWER OF THE REDEEMER MANIFEST IN THE LIFE OF BELIEVERS

In this study it has been clearly made out, we believe, that, from Paul's point of view, man's salvation is eschatological, cosmic and dynamic. It is eschatological because it means, fundamentally, God's deliverance of men from the impending wrath, his transforming of them into his own likeness and nature, and his sharing with them his functions as ruler and judge of the universe.[184] All these experiences pertain to the future. It is cosmic and dynamic, because, in order for God to accomplish these results, it was necessary for him through the exercise of superhuman power ($\delta\acute{v}\nu\alpha\mu\iota\varsigma$), to rescue men from the control of the Evil Powers of the cosmos. As long as men were under the control of these Powers, they would be the victims of the impending wrath, because primarily this wrath was

[184] I Cor. 6: 2, 3.

directed against these Powers. Secondarily, it
embraced all who were associated with them in
opposition to God. Furthermore, as long as
men were subject to these Powers, they would do
their bidding, and could not of course attain unto
the likeness and nature of God.

This eschatological character of salvation, and
particularly the shortness of the time to elapse
before the Parousia of the Son of God, when
salvation would be complete, had a pronounced
effect upon the Apostle's view of the social order. He regarded it as unwise to make new
social adjustments, believing it to be proper after
conversion, to continue in, and to use, the same
relationships in which one was before conversion.
If one were a slave before conversion, he was
not to take steps for his emancipation, even if
freedom were a possibility for him. On the
other hand, if he were a freeman when he became a believer he was not to sell himself into
slavery.[185] The same principle obtained with reference to marriage. If one were unmarried or had
lost husband, or wife, it were best not to marry.
However, if one were already married at the time

[185] I Cor. 7:18-24.

of becoming a believer, it were best to continue the marriage relation, especially in view of the fact that it gave the believing husband or wife an excellent opportunity to labor for the salvation of the unbelieving partner.[186]

But, it may be asked, did Paul transfer all the benefits of redemption to the future life? Did salvation mean little more for this life than a waiting for the coming transformation? By no means. The life of the believer here in this world was interpreted as a thorough-going manifestation and product of that cosmic power of God by which the redemption of the world and of men was being wrought out. Since man's salvation is involved in the ultimate overthrow of Satan and his hosts, the life of the believer becomes a part of the cosmic conflict. God is still the protagonist on the side of the good. Just as, before the redemptive work of Jesus, men played a secondary part in the world's drama, so, after that work has been performed, as it was in the death and resurrection of Jesus,

---

[186] I Cor. 7:1-17, 25-40. Paul regards his directions in these matters as being reasonable in view of the shortness of the time preceding the Parousia (I Cor. 7:29-31).

men are still the agents, or media, through whom the chieftains, God and Satan, operate. The believers are ranged on the side of God. Paul is nothing and Apollos is nothing—simply ministers through whose instrumentality the Corinthians made the transfer of their allegiance from Satan to God, and that only as God ordained. Paul planted and Apollos watered, but God gave the increase. Believers are workers together with God, not simply for their individual salvation, but for the successful carrying out of God's entire program of world redemption, and their reward is determined by the manner in which their work stands the fiery test of the last day.[187]

It is true, not only that one takes his first steps in the Christian life through the power, or calling of God,[188] but also that, having entered upon it, he is guarded from evil, or the Evil One, by God.[189] The supplying of the Spirit to believers is the work of God, as is the working of miracles by believers.[190] The bodies of believers are not their own to do with them as they please.

[187] 1 Cor. 3:5-15.
[188] 1 Cor. 1:9; 7:17-24; Gal. 5:8; 1 Thes. 2:12; 4:7; 5:24.
[189] 2 Thes. 3:3.
[190] Gal. 3:5.

They belong to God. They are his property, having been purchased by him. They are the temples in which he dwells through the Spirit.[191] Even in physical weakness, in persecutions, distresses, and when plagued by some disease operating as a messenger of Satan to beat him down, Paul could exult in the divine power, which made him strong, even superior to his foes.[192]

The thorough participation of the believer in the redemptive process of the cosmos is expressed in many ways by Paul, chief among them being the following expressions: in Christ, the Holy Spirit, freedom from Sin, the Charismata of the Spirit, faith, love, hope. To understand Paul's conception of the Christian life one must penetrate the real significance of these expressions.

Judged by its New Testament usage, the expression, *in Christ,* is distinctively, though not exclusively, Pauline.[193] By it Paul brings out the

[191] 1 Cor. 6:12-20.

[192] 2 Cor. 12:7-10; 13:3-5; Phil. 4:11-13.

[193] According to Deissmann, it and its equivalents, such as *in Jesus, in the Lord, in him, in whom* (=Christ), and the like, occur 196 times in the New Testament, 164 times in the Pauline letters. It does not occur in the Synoptic Gospels, James, Second Peter, Jude, or Hebrews. It is

cosmic and dynamic union which subsists between the believer and the Redeemer. Christ actually enters into, and is formed in the believer.[194] In consequence of this union, the believer, while in the body, lives a supernatural life. He no longer lives; Christ lives in him.[195] The life of the natural man has ceased to exist for him. This life of the natural man has its dynamic source in a cosmic Power, or personality, namely, Sin. The life of the believer has its dynamic source in a cosmic Power, or personality also, namely, Christ, who is superior to Sin. This superiority of Christ over Sin was demonstrated in his death and resurrection. In his death on the cross he died to Sin once, and overcame Sin. In the cosmic, life-giving power, which caused him to live again, he lives in unison with God's world-purpose.[196] He is the dispenser of God's power for the ends of redemp-

---

found eight times in Acts and First Peter, twenty-four times in the Johannine writings, including Revelation. *Die neutestamentliche Formel "in Christo Jesu,"* Marburg, 1892, 1 ff.

[194] Gal. 4:19.

[195] Gal. 2:17-21. Whether or not Paul's ideal was realized by believers our study does not attempt to determine.

[196] Rom. 6:9-11.

tion.   Likewise, the believer, in identifying himself with Christ by faith, dies to the cosmic Power, Sin.[197]   By virtue of the superior cosmic power, with which he makes connection in his union with the Redeemer, the believer lives a life of triumph over Sin.

It follows, of course, that such a union with Christ as is expressed in the formula, *in Christ,* was not in any sense incidental to the Christian life.   It is not to be put down simply to the account of Paul's mysticism.   It is not supplementary to his idea of righteousness, a Pauline idiosyncrasy, so to speak.   It is absolutely fundamental and necessary to his redemptive program. "We live," he writes to the Thessalonians, "if ye stand *in the Lord.*" [198]   The inference is plain.   If the Thessalonians were not *in the Lord,* then they were lost, and Paul's labors in their behalf were fruitless.   In this absolute necessity of being in Christ, we have a partial ex-

---

[197] In Gal. 2:19, Paul says he "died to law."   In Rom. 6:6, he says "Our old man was crucified (with Christ) in order that the body of Sin might be destroyed, that we might no longer be slaves to Sin."   Dying to Law and dying to Sin are synonymous expressions.
[198] I Thes. 3:8.

planation at least of Paul's impetuous and un-
compromising method of handling a case of de-
fection from Christ, as in Galatia, or of sin, as in
Corinth.   There could be no compromise, because the difference between him and his opponents was not one of opinion simply.   To take
the course contemplated by them would inevit-
ably result in severing that union between themselves and Christ on which their salvation de-
pended.   This being Paul's point of view, we
can understand why he should become vehement
in his efforts to prevent his converts from taking
this fatal step.[199]

[199] It will perhaps already have been observed that we
have given to the formula *in Christ* a significance differing
from that which Deissmann adopted, as a result of his
excellent study of the phrase. He considers that it char-
acterizes the *local* relation which is established between
the Christian and Christ, Christ being regarded as the
element within which the Christian lives, and within which
all the manifestations of the unique Christian life find
expression. Deissmann believes it to be impossible to
decide with certainty whether the local idea is real or
simply rhetorical, but inclines to the first alternative. In
either case, he regards the formula as the peculiarly
Pauline expression for the most intimate communion
thinkable of the Christian with the living Christ. Con-
cerning the actual character of this communion with
Christ, Deissmann holds, the formula furnishes us nothing conclusive (*Die neutestamentliche Formel "in Christo*

In the phrases, *in the Spirit, in the Holy Spirit,* etc., Paul expresses substantially the same idea as in the formula, *in Christ.*[200]   He uses the term, Spirit, or Holy Spirit, in a variety of expressions such as *walking in the Spirit, led by the Spirit, having the Spirit, being in the Spirit, the Spirit being in one, receiving the Spirit, living by the Spirit.*   In such expressions Paul uses the words Spirit and Christ without any apparent difference in meaning.   In the Spirit the believer has the same cosmic, dynamic power for the overcoming of his foes, as he has in God, or in

Jesu," Marburg, 1892, pp. 81, 82, 97, 98).   We have given it a cosmic and dynamic significance.   As such it is not primarily "local."   Nor is the idea fundamentally that of communion.   Furthermore, Christ is not regarded as "the element, within which the Christian lives, etc."   He is regarded as the divine Redeemer, the Son of God, the channel for the conveying to men of the cosmic redemptive power of God, upon which power man's salvation depends.   It may not be possible to translate the phrase satisfactorily, but such a combination as, *in the power of and in union and communion with Christ,* seems to approach its meaning very closely.   Power, union and communion are here given in the order of their importance, the primary idea being power.

[200] For the parallel citations see Deissmann, *Die neutestamentliche Formel "in Christo Jesu,"* Marburg, 1892, 85 ff.   Cf. Gunkel, *Die Wirkungen des heiligen Geistes,* etc., Göttingen, 1888, a.a. O., 97 ff.

Christ. Through the power of the Spirit, just as through the power of Christ, the believer lives the ethical life, without which he cannot be saved.[201]

Enough has already been said to indicate that, from Paul's point of view, the life of the believer should be a sinless one.[202] We may go further and say that, for him, it was unthinkable that it should be otherwise. When he asks, "Shall we continue in Sin, that grace may abound?" He replies: "Far be it!" He then proceeds to show why it is impossible. His argument runs as follows: In his death on the cross, Jesus died to Sin once and for all, and thereby conquered Sin. In his resurrection, he asserted once and for all his independence of and his superiority to Sin. Thenceforth he lives to God, which means that Sin has no longer any influence over him. Now, we as believers have

[201] Gal. 5:16-26; Rom. 8:3-9.

[202] To this conclusion Wernle came, as a result of his special study of this question: "That the Christian attitude demands no further contact with sin, that the Christian is a sinless man, and as such appears shortly before God at the Judgment Day, is the result of this investigation." *Der Christ und die Sünde bei Paulus,* Leipzig, 1897, 126 f.

re-enacted this drama in our own lives. We have been crucified with Christ. In that crucifixion of our former self we overcame Sin, as far as we are concerned, just as Jesus overcame Sin for the sake of all men. In consequence we are no longer to be enslaved to Sin. But just as Jesus was raised to a new life, so have we been also. We must reckon ourselves, therefore, to be dead to Sin, but alive to God in Christ Jesus. Sin, therefore, is not to reign as a sovereign in our mortal bodies, forcing us to obey its behests. We are not to present our bodies to Sin, for service, but to God, as those who are alive from the dead and therefore superior to Sin inasmuch as Death and Sin are allied in their antagonism to men.[203]

This insistence upon the sinless life was not only a logical necessity in Paul's philosophy of salvation, but, as already indicated, it was an absolute pre-requisite to the inheritance of the future blessedness. Paul keeps this idea constantly before the minds of his readers.[204]   The

[203] Rom. 6:1-14.   Cf. also 1 Thes. 3:12; 4:1-6; 1 Cor. 5:3-13; Col. 3:5-12; Eph. 4:17-24.
[204] Rom. 6:12-14, 22, 23; 7:5, 6; 8:1-17; 1 Cor. 5:3-5.

final destiny of the believer will be determined, not by the fact that he honored Christ, during his earthly life, by assenting to his messiahship and divine sonship, but by the life he has led. God cannot, for our special benefit, even if we have believed on his Son, alter the principles of the cosmic contest, which he is waging with his cosmic foes.   The sinful life is *prima facie* evidence of alliance with Sin, God's enemy.[205]   In order to decide one's fate at the Judgment, it will only be necessary to establish the fact that he has lived a sinful life.   Such a person cannot inherit the kingdom of God.[206]   This is not unfair on God's part,[207] since in the cosmic power which he has made available in Christ, or in the Holy Spirit, everyone has at command the means for living the sinless life, and thus being worthy of the inheritance which awaits the sons of God. If men fail to make use of this power, they cannot hold God responsible for their final destruction.   God has done his part in providing the

[205] Rom. 6:15-23.
[206] 1 Cor. 6:9, 10; Gal. 5:19-21; Eph. 5:5.
[207] Rom. 3:5.

means of salvation. Each one must make use of them for himself.[208]

The gift of the Spirit was primarily, of course, for the believer's own salvation. But Paul recognizes a secondary effect of the Spirit's presence and power in the life of the believer, in the Charismata, or gifts of the Spirit. These Charismata fall into two groups. There are gifts which have to do with the edification of the church and with the conversion of unbelievers, such as the word of wisdom, the word of knowledge, faith, prophecy, discerning of spirits, speaking with tongues, interpreting of tongues. Again, there are gifts which give evidence of the believers' superiority over the demonic Powers in that they are able to perform miracles, particularly in the healing of diseases.[209]

Looked at from the human side of the problem, so to speak, the Christian life is marked by three outstanding characteristics—faith, love, hope. Paul was given to grouping these to-

[208] As salvation is determined finally on the basis of conduct, in the earthly life, so the extent of one's rewards is determined by his success in turning men to righteousness.

[209] I Cor. 12:1–13:2; 14:1-40.

gether.[210]   Faith is the act wherein the believer transfers his allegiance from Satan to God.   On its negative side, this transfer of allegiance is called repentance.   On its positive side, it is called faith, or, verbally, to believe on, or in (Greek, *into*) Christ.   Faith in Christ is an act of self-commitment to Christ for salvation, an enlistment with him in the cosmic struggle.   In believing on Christ one appropriates the divine power, which is at work for the redemption of the world.   Because of this fact it constitutes the saving act pre-eminently.[211]   Since man's salvation is inseparably connected with the redemption of the cosmos, he must be indissolubly united with the power which is to effect this redemption.   This is the meaning of the question, "Who shall separate us from the love (equivalent here to power) of Christ?   Shall tribulation,

[210] I Thes. 1:3; 5:8; I Cor. 13:13; Col. 1:4, 5. Cf. 2 Thes. 1:3.

[211] The criterion by which one is to know whether or not he is saved is the presence or absence of the Spirit (Gal. 3:2).   It is through faith that the Spirit is received, and the evidence of the Spirit is detected by manifestations of cosmic power, as in the working of miracles (Gal. 3:5), or in the freedom of the life from the dominating influence of Sin (Gal. 5:16-25).

or anguish, or persecution, or famine, or nakedness, or peril, or sword? . . . Nay, in all these
things we are more than conquerors through
him that loved us. For I am persuaded that
neither death, nor life, nor angels, nor principalities, nor things present, nor things to come, nor
powers, nor height, nor depth, nor any other
creature, shall be able to separate us from the
love (or power) of God, which is in Christ Jesus
our Lord." [212]

Paul's favorite expression for the ethical life,
on its positive side, is love. This quality, or
virtue, embraces all that can be desired in conduct. He who loves fulfills the requirements of
the law, and meets all God's demands.[213]   Paul
cannot urge on his converts too strongly the in-
junction to love; to find indisputable evidence of
love in them gives him the greatest joy.[214]   Love
exhibits itself in self-denying regard for the
needs, scruples and desires of others.[215]   It is
the norm of the life of those who are striving
for salvation, because it corresponds with the na-

[212] Rom. 8: 35-39.
[213] Rom. 13: 8-10; Gal. 5: 14.
[214] I Thes. 4: 9-12.
[215] I Cor. 8: 13; 10: 24—11: 1; 11: 17—22, 33, 34.

ture of Him to whom they have committed
themselves for this salvation. In his great provision for man's salvation God gave evidence of
his unbounded love for man.[216]   He revealed
himself as a God of love. It follows that those
who have made common cause with him and are
identified with him in the carrying forward of
the cosmic program must live in unison with his
nature. To use another figure, believers are
God's sons. He has sent forth his Spirit into
their hearts assuring them of the fact. Being
sons, they partake of the nature of the Father,
which is love. To live the life of love is therefore not only necessary but natural to the believer. Deeds of love spring by a law of the
Spirit from the life of the believers as a normal
product, as fruit.[217]   Love is an expression of
the cosmic power of the same Spirit which produces the Charismata in believers; only love is
far more to be desired than any of these striking
demonstrations of the Spirit's power.[218]   It is
the living out of the will, purpose, and, we

[216] Rom. 5 : 6-11 ; Gal. 2 : 20; Eph. 5 : 1, 2.
[217] Gal. 5 : 16-26.
[218] I Cor. 12 : 31b-13 : 13.

might almost say, life of God in the life of believers. This fact, coupled with the other, already referred to, namely, that the life of love
will certainly stand successfully the tests of the
Judgment Day, may help to explain why Paul,
despite the significance which he attaches to
faith, declares love to be greater than faith.[219]

   The importance which Paul attaches to hope is
not, as might appear on first thought, exaggerated. The explanation of this importance is
found in the eschatological character of salvation. Only when this age is past and the coming age has set in will the saved enter upon
the full realization of the blessings of salvation. The conditions of the present life are undesirable. One is beset on every hand by enemies, visible and invisible. If salvation affords
nothing better than what this life offers, it is not
worth while. "If for this life only we have our
hope in Christ, we are of all men most miser-
able." [220]   But hope holds out something more
than the experiences of this life. It reaches forward beyond this life into the future, and makes

[219] I Cor. 13:13.
[220] I Cor. 15:19; cf. also vss. 31, 32.

the eschatological experiences so real and certain that it becomes possible for one to look with indifference upon the sufferings of this present life, since they are not to be compared with the glory which shall be revealed in us hereafter.[221]

These three characteristics of the Christian life, namely, faith, hope and love, constitute in Paul's thinking a triangular foundation, on which, if a man rests, his salvation is assured. He can be said to be saved now, in this life, not because the present experience actually constitutes a completed salvation, but because it constitutes so thorough-going a certainty of it, that, by an accommodation of terms, the future reality may be put for the present promise and assurance of that reality. Through faith he is united with the world's Redeemer, and has at his command the unlimited redemptive power of God. Through a life of love he gives expression to this divine power and to the divine nature, which he shares. Being thus in his spiritual nature a son of God, he must inherit the blessings which God has prepared for his sons. Through the exercise of hope, by means of which he contem-

[221] Rom. 8: 18, 19; 2 Cor. 4: 17.

plates the glorious transformation which is soon to come, he is enabled, rising superior to his present adversities, to remain faithful to the calling to an eschatological salvation, into which he has been called by God in Christ Jesus.

CHAPTER V

THE REDEEMER AND THE CONSUMMATION OF THE REDEMPTIVE PROGRAM

As we have seen, Paul's interest was primarily in that part of the redemptive program which had to do with man's salvation. The questions which bulk large in his letters are such as have to do with the thraldom from which man is saved by the power of God, the future blessedness which is assured him in salvation, the means by which salvation is made a possibility, and the life which the saved lived here on earth while awaiting their complete redemption, namely, the apocalypse of the sons of God. On the more philosophical questions touching the redemption of the cosmos itself Paul has less to say. He tells us comparatively little regarding the nature of the Godhead or the relation of God the Father, God the Son and God the Spirit to the universe of matter. He does little more than name the ranks of the intermediary beings, with which the underworld and the super-terrestrial regions are inhabited. Little is disclosed of their nature and functions. What the future of the whole is to be is sketched only in the boldest outlines. Yet his utterances on some of these points are sufficiently suggestive and explicit to enable us to follow, with some feeling of certainty, the main currents of his thought.

His favorite designations for the Redeemer are Jesus, Jesus Christ, Lord, Son of God. There is a striking correspondence between some of the attributes and functions which Paul ascribes to Jesus and those which are ascribed to the Son of Man in Jewish apocalyptical literature. At the same time, Paul does not use the term Son of Man at all. This fact has been adduced by some writers in support of the theory that the term Son of Man was not a current messianic title in the time of Paul or of Jesus, and that it was introduced into the Gospels a considerable time after Paul, as a result of its use in Christian apocalypses. The main line of argument in support of this theory is linguistic, and is based on the contention that the Aramaic equivalent of the term Son of Man, viz., *bar nash* or *bar nasha,* had no titular significance, and that it meant simply "man" or "the man." This much discussed question is too large to be entered upon here. It is sufficient to point out that those who deny the possibility of a titular character attaching to the term encounter serious difficulties, and their arguments have not thus far been generally convincing. We would point out in particular that perhaps too much weight has been attached to the fact that Paul does not use the term. In explanation of this several reasons suggest themselves. First, while Paul ascribes to Jesus nearly every important characteristic which apocalypticism gave to the Son of Man, these all taken together do not make up the Christ of Paul. To Paul Christ is virtually all that the Son of Man is, and much more, for in addition to having the apocalyptical functions, which were ascribed to the Son of Man, Christ had died and risen from the dead in order to redeem men. As these facts were all-important for Paul's theology, to have designated him the Son of Man would have been to contract and circumscribe the Christ of his faith. Furthermore, the

term Son of Man was more or less indefinite as
far as the identity of the person so designated
was concerned.[222]   Regarding the identity of
Jesus there seems to have been no question, in
the time of Paul.   Again, it is easily conceivable
that the term Son of Man was not well adapted
to Paul's Gentile mission.   It contained a suggestion which was at variance with his high
Christology.   For him Christ was not primarily
the Son of Man, that is, of humanity, but the
Son of God.   To be sure, he had been born of a
woman, and was clothed with human flesh, but
his life in the flesh, as we shall see presently,
was only a brief moment in his eternal, cosmic
existence.   It is not surprising, therefore, that
Paul, while placing Jesus in the framework of
Jewish apocalypticism, uses a Christological terminology which is more definite and clear than
the term Son of Man and which expresses more
truly Paul's enlarged conception of Jesus.   The
term Son of God, we are warranted in believing,

[222] For example, "The multitude therefore answered him,
We have heard from the law that the Christ abides forever, and how sayest thou that the Son of Man must be
lifted up?   Who is this Son of Man?"   Jn. 12:34.

was the term which most fully reproduced his thought. His other favorite terms, Jesus, Jesus Christ, Lord, all carried with them the same connotation as did the term Son of God.

The Redeemer of men was, to Paul's thinking, a cosmic figure, having the nature, attributes and functions of God. He had pre-existed with God before the worlds were made, and had had a share in their making.[223] To him was committed the task of overthrowing the Evil Powers of the universe and thereby redeeming it, or restoring it to God the Father. This redemptive work was inaugurated in the sending by the Father of the Son to earth to make possible man's salvation. This took place in an epochal hour of cosmic history, that is, when the fullness of the time came.[224]

That Paul attributed to Jesus an earthly existence is fully made out, for he witnesses both to his birth [225] and to his historical death.[226] He knows also of his betrayal and of his participa-

[223] Phil. 2:5-8; Col. 1:15-17.
[224] Gal. 4:4; Eph. 1:9, 10.
[225] Rom. 1:3; 9:5; Gal. 4:4.
[226] 1 Thes. 2:15; Gal. 5:11; 6:12, 14; Phil. 2:8. Cf. Case, *The Historicity of Jesus,* Chicago, 1912, Chap. VI.

tion in the Last Supper.[227]   Yet how meager are
these references to the matchless life of Jesus.
One could hardly excuse an indifferent historian
for passing over such a career without more extended notice, how much less an enthusiastic de-
votee like Paul.   Furthermore, it is evident that
the things he does mention are not given for any
human or historical interest.   They all belong to
theology, and constitute momenta in the world's
redemptive program.   This inference is clear
enough, but it is further supported by Paul's explicit statement that he ceased to know Christ
after the flesh.[228]   This means that the earthly,
historical Jesus had no vital significance for him.

But why should the birth and death of Jesus
have greater theological significance for Paul
than his life and teaching did?   For the modern
mind, uninfluenced by Paul, it is not so.   The
reverse is more apt to be the case, particularly
if only that feature of the birth, which Paul
brings out, is dwelt on.   For it must be borne in
mind that Paul does not witness to the virgin
birth of Jesus.   What he emphasizes is that

[227] 1 Cor. 11:23-26.   [228] 2 Cor. 5:16.

Christ was born under the law, born of a woman[229] and that he was in the likeness of sinful flesh.[230] Just why these particular facts should be of supreme religious significance it is difficult for the modern mind to conceive. The explanation lies in the fact that we touch here a very peculiar feature of Paul's theology, one probably that will become clearer to us as we learn more of the religious thought of his day, particularly in the realm of the mystery-religions. He discerned a pronounced correspondence, or parallelism, between the ends sought in redemption and the means necessary to attain those ends. Christ was to redeem man from Sin and Death. It was necessary that he should become, in some sense, sin, although he knew no sin.[231] By being made in the likeness of sinful flesh he condemned Sin in the flesh.[232] By becoming subject to

[229] Gal. 4:4.

[230] Rom. 8:3. In Rom. 1:3 he is declared to be "of the seed of David according to the flesh," but no significance is assigned to this fact by Paul. Likewise the author of 2 Tim. 2:8 writes: "Remember Jesus Christ risen from the dead, of the seed of David, according to my gospel." But again no use is made of the fact of Jesus' descent from David.

[231] 2 Cor. 5:21.

[232] Rom. 8:3.

Death he redeemed men from Death, a thing which the agents of Death did not forecast, for, had they done so, they would not have crucified the Lord of Glory.[233]   He was to save men from Law, another cosmic Power.   He, in consequence, was born under Law, and somehow, mysterious no doubt to us, he redeemed us from Law, its slavery and curse.[234]

The conclusion seems unavoidable that Paul viewed the earthly life of Jesus not as different from but as a part of his age-long cosmic existence.   It had for him no historical meaning except from the standpoint of cosmic history.[235] But if it was insignificant for earthly history, it was all-important for the history of the cosmos. For in his death and resurrection Jesus admin-

[233] 1 Cor. 2 : 7, 8.

[234] Gal. 4 : 4, 5.

[235] It is possible that the paucity of Paul's references to the earthly Jesus may be in a measure attributable to his unwillingness to concede to his Judaizing opponents any advantage which they might get out of such references. It was one of their principal contentions that their gospel represented the thought of the original Apostles, who had seen and associated with Jesus. They discredited Paul and his gospel because he had not seen Jesus. Paul felt compelled to meet that argument, and did so by claiming to have seen the risen Jesus. Whether the turn Paul took here was dialectically justifiable or not we need not con-

istered to Satan and his hosts an initial and partial defeat, which was to be followed up until the victory was made complete.

While man has his part to play, as we have shown already, and while, through the Spirit, God also takes part in the earthly conflict, rendering indispensable aid to those who commit themselves to him,[236] the cosmic struggle, in its larger proportions, is really carried on in the super-terrestrial regions. Thither Christ has gone by means of his ascension. Exalted to the right hand of God on high, he is given a place superior to all the intermediary beings of the universe.[237] There he is to reign until the work of redemption is complete, that is, until all the cosmic enemies of God have been vanquished. For he must reign until he puts all his enemies beneath his feet, all those hosts of intermediary

sider. The situation is what we are interested in. It may explain in part Paul's failure to ascribe to the earthly life of Jesus that religious value which the modern man finds in it. But if it constitutes an explanation at all it must be only a partial explanation. The fuller explanation must be found in Paul's fundamental conception of the redemptive work of Christ.

[236] Rom. 8: 26, 27.
[237] Eph. 1: 20, 21; 4:15; Phil. 2:5-11; Col. 1:17-19.

beings, such as Rule, Authority and Power. The
last of these to be completely overthrown is
Death. Then comes the *end,* that is, the end of
Christ's redemptive work, the end of his reign.
The redemption of the universe complete, all
God's enemies destroyed, Christ the Son turns
over to the Father the redeemed universe, the
Son himself to take a place subordinate to the
Father, in order that God the Father may be all
in all.[238]

Just what the future condition of the earth,
considered apart from the rest of the cosmos, is
to be is not altogether clear. The passage just
cited from Corinthians seems to throw no light
on the question. A corresponding passage in
Romans seems to point in the direction of a re-
habilitated earth, wherein the adverse Powers
of Evil will not exert their baleful influence.
Although this conclusion does not rest on specific
statements, it is strongly supported by the con-
sciousness which Paul seems to have of the fact,
detecting it apparently by experience, that the
whole creation groaneth and travaileth in pain
until now, awaiting its deliverance which will

[238] I Cor. 15:20-28.

come simultaneously with the transformation of the sons of God.[239]

This transformation of the sons of God was the logical outcome of the divine life which the believer entered upon here. The cosmic victory over his foes which was won for him by the Redeemer in his death and resurrection was sufficient for the needs of this life, since it enabled the believer to live superior to Sin and thus insured him ultimate victory over Death, eternal death being the wages of Sin. Once emancipated from Sin by the power of the Redeemer, and subsequently remaining free from Sin through his own moral earnestness, which was made effective through the use of the divine power mediated through the Spirit, the believer lived in confident expectation of a complete and final triumph over Death, or in other words of a glorious immortality. The experience of salvation which this earthly life afforded him, while it was actual and truly real, was nevertheless only partial, provisional and proleptical. Paul reckoned that the sufferings of this present time were not worthy to be compared with the glory

[239] Rom. 8:19-22.

which shall be revealed in us.[240]   He considered
that the light afflictions, which characterize the
earthly life, work out for us a far more exceeding and eternal weight of glory, while we look
not at the things which are seen but at the eternal things which are not seen.[241]   Even the word
righteousness (δικαιοσύνη) Paul associates closely
with these experiences of the future life: "That
I may gain Christ and be found in him, not
having a righteousness which is of my own
achieving through keeping the law, but the
righteousness which is by faith in Christ, the
righteousness which comes from God as its
source upon the basis of faith, in order that I
may know him and the power of his resurrection and the fellowship of his sufferings, being
conformed to his death, if by any means I may
attain unto the resurrection from the dead." [242]

Despite the fact that the life in Christ here on
earth was so realistic to Paul that he could de-
clare that he no longer lived, but that Christ lived
in him and that the life which he lived he lived
in the power of Christ, he nevertheless affirmed

[240] Rom. 8:18.   [241] 2 Cor. 4: 17, 18.
[242] Phil. 3:8b-11.

most emphatically that this was by no means all
of salvation, as the following statement shows:
"Not that I have already attained, or am already made perfect, but I press on, if so be that
I may lay hold on that for which I was laid
hold on by Christ Jesus. Brethren, I count not
myself yet to have laid hold: but one thing, for-
getting the things which are behind and stretch-
ing forward to the things which are before, I
press on toward the goal unto the prize of the
calling of God in Christ Jesus which is on
high." [243]

The earthly life of the believer was passed in
hourly expectancy of those future events which
would signalize the completion of Redemption.
Each day brought salvation nearer. "And moreover, knowing the time (the cosmic moment
when "the present age" ceases and "the coming
age" begins) that it is already the hour for you
to awake from sleep; for now is our salvation
nearer than when we believed. The night ("the
present age" of darkness) [244] is far spent; the
day ("the coming age" of light) is at hand.

[243] Phil. 3:12-14.
[244] 1 Thes. 5:4, 5; 1 Cor. 4:5; Col. 1:13; Eph. 5:8.

Let us therefore cast off the works of darkness, and let us put on the weapons of light.[245] Let us conduct ourselves becomingly, as in the day, not in rioting and drunkenness, not in unchastity and wantonness, not in strife and envying. But put ye on the Lord Jesus Christ, and make no provision for the flesh, to fulfill its desires." [246]

Man's salvation in its full realization was inextricably bound up with those cosmic happenings which were to mark the consummation of the world's redemption. Man's salvation could not become complete until those events took place. Chief among these were the Parousia, the Resurrection, and the Judgment with its determining of the destinies of the good and the evil.

For the idea of the Redeemer's coming to earth Paul used a variety of expressions.[247] The

[245] Note the military term. The figure seems to be that of a sleeping soldier, who on awaking at the dawn of day, quickly lays aside his night garments and puts on his armor in readiness for service. For the believer this military equipment would appear to be the Lord Jesus Christ (Rom. 13:14).

[246] Rom. 13:11-14.

[247] Our expression Second Coming or Second Advent is strictly speaking not warranted by Paul's usage, possibly

chief of these are: the Parousia,[248] the Day, or
the Day of the Lord, of Christ, etc.,[249] the
Apocalypse of our Lord Jesus Christ [250] and the
Apocalypse of our Lord from heaven.[251] In the
Pastorals and once in 2 Thessalonians the word
appearing (ἐπιφάνεια) is found.[252] The outstanding features of the Parousia are: that Christ will
descend on the clouds from heaven with a shout,
with the voice of the archangel and with the
trump of God.[253] He will be accompanied by
the angels of his power in flaming fire.[254]

The significance of the Parousia is that it constitutes the supreme manifestation of God's
power over his cosmic enemies, in particular, the
most formidable of them all—Death. In a moment, in the twinkling of an eye at the last
trump, the dead in Christ, those who sleep in

not by the remainder of the New Testament. Cf. W. B.
Smith, *Der vorchristliche Jesus,* Giessen, 1906.

[248] I Cor. 15:23; I Thes. 2:19; 3:13; 4:15; 5:23; 2 Thes.
2: 1, 9.

[249] I Cor. 1:8; 5:5; 2 Cor. 1:14; Phil. 1:6, 10; 2:16; I
Thes. 5: 2, 4; 2 Thes. 1:10; 2:2.

[250] I Cor. 1:7.

[251] 2 Thes. 1:7.

[252] 2 Thes. 2:8; I Tim. 6:14; 2 Tim. 1:10; 4:1; Tit. 2:13.

[253] I Thes. 4:16.

[254] 2 Thes. 1: 7, 8. Cf. Isa. 66:15.

him, shall rise incorruptible, which is equivalent
to saying that thenceforth they are freed from
Death, and out of reach of his destructive
power.[255]

Paul's view of salvation as a rescue from the
Evil Powers and as an impartation to the believer of the superior power of God for the
overcoming of these evil forces would logically
require that only the believers in Jesus, that is,
those who have appropriated this power will
rise, or come back from the abode of the dead.
One cannot be certain as to what Paul thought
on this point. In so far as he has expressed himself he seems to be consistent with the logic of
his system. He does not represent the wicked
as rising at the coming of the Lord. He distinctly says that it is "those who are asleep
through Jesus" whom God will bring with Jesus.

[255] I Cor. 15:52. In I Thes. 4:14 the language is: "If
we believe that Jesus died and rose again, so shall God
lead ($\check{\alpha}\xi\epsilon\iota$) with him (Jesus) those who sleep through ($\delta\iota\grave{\alpha}$)
Jesus." The meaning seems to be that God will, by the
aid of Jesus, or in company with Jesus, lead back from
the abode of the dead and consequently from the power of
Death those who have been asleep through Jesus, and
therefore still within his power, and presumably beyond
the complete power of Death.

God will make alive the mortal bodies of men, provided the Spirit of him who raised Jesus from the dead dwells in them, for it is through the power of this Spirit that their bodies are made thus alive.[256] If in 1 Cor. 15:52 Paul does not explicitly indicate that the dead who shall rise at Christ's coming are believers, he does so implicitly. The passage shows that he has in mind only those who are united with Christ. He divides them into two classes, those who have died and those who are still alive at Jesus' coming. Where Paul says that the dead shall rise incorruptible, he can only mean the dead in Christ.

Those who are alive at the Parousia triumph over Death, just as those do who are brought back from Death's abode by the power of God. They shall be transformed. "This corruptible (the part of us now subject to Death's power) must put on incorruption, and this mortal (equivalent to corruptible) must put on immortality. But when this corruptible shall have put on incorruption, and this mortal shall have put on immortality, then shall come to pass the say-

[256] Rom. 8:11.

ing that is written, Death is swallowed up in victory." [257]

How this is accomplished Paul does not indicate further than to say that it is the work of God through our Lord Jesus Christ. The exultant language in which this thought is expressed goes to show that in this particular achievement of the Redeemer Paul saw the crowning act in man's salvation. "O Death, where is thy victory? O Death, where is thy sting? The sting of Death is Sin and the power of Sin is the Law, but thanks be to God who giveth us the victory (over all three of these cosmic foes of man) through our Lord Jesus Christ." [258] This transformation of those who are alive at the Parousia Paul designates as a mystery (μυστήριον). If there was a body of esoteric teaching in Paul's gospel, the probability is that the doctrine of the resurrection and the metamorphosis of believers at the Parousia constituted an important part of it. But this is only to say in another way that Paul's gospel, or doctrine of salvation, had for its central idea the overcoming of Death by

[257] I Cor. 15:51-54.
[258] I Cor. 15:55-57. Cf. Isa. 25:8; Hos. 13:14.

man through the power of the Redeemer Jesus Christ at his Parousia. Through this power man secured a blessed immortality. In brief that is Paul's gospel. That is what he means by salvation.

It follows of necessity that those who are alive at the Parousia but are not in Christ are destroyed. "When they are saying, Peace and safety, then sudden destruction cometh upon them . . . and they shall by no means escape." [259] The exact nature of this destruction it is not easy to determine. It is referred to as death.[260] If this expression is interpreted absolutely, it may be given the meaning of annihilation. But more probably it is to be interpreted relatively, and by contrast with the term "eternal life," which occurs along with it. Eternal life refers, not simply to eternal existence, but to the joys and blessings which characterize eternal life. So death may refer, not to absolute destruction, but to a condition of relative unhappiness and misery. Paul probably gave expres-

[259] 1 Thes. 5:3. Cf. Rom. 2:9; 6:23; 1 Cor. 3:17; 5:5; 6:9; 15:50; Phil. 1:28; 3:19.
[260] Rom. 6:21, 23.

sion to this idea when he declared that the
wicked shall not inherit the Kingdom of God.[261]
What is meant by this may be seen in part from
the passage: "Or despiseth thou the riches of
his goodness and forbearance and longsuffering,
not knowing that the goodness of God leadeth
thee to repentance? But after thy hardness and
impenitent heart treasurest up for thyself wrath
in a day of wrath and revelation of the righteous judgment of God; who will render to every
man according to his works: to them that by
patience in well-doing seek for glory and honor
and incorruption, eternal life: but unto them that
are factious, and obey not the truth, but obey
unrighteousness, shall be wrath and indignation,
tribulation and anguish, upon every soul of man
that worketh evil, of the Jew first and also of
the Greek; but glory and honor and peace to
every man that worketh good, to the Jew first
and also to the Greek; for there is no respect of
persons with God." [262]

The terms, wrath, indignation, tribulation and
anguish are put over against such terms as
glory, honor, incorruption and eternal life, and

[261] 1 Cor. 6:9, 10; 15:50.   [262] Rom. 2:4 11.

therefore express the misery of those who fail to inherit the blessings of the saved. Beyond this Paul does not seem to go. Even in his most descriptive utterance on the subject he seems to limit himself to terms indicative of failure to attain to the joys of the blessed: "And to you that are afflicted rest with us, at the revelation of the Lord Jesus from heaven with the angels of his power in flaming fire, rendering vengeance to them that know not God, and to them that obey not the gospel of our Lord Jesus: who shall suffer punishment, even eternal destruction from the face of the Lord and from the glory of his might, when he shall come to be glorified in his saints and to be marveled at in all them that believed . . . in that day." [263]

It appears that Paul in his references to the future state of the wicked confines himself to the use of general terms, which are for the most part negative in character. There is no reference to Gehenna, or to a lake of fire, as is the case in the Synoptic Gospels. This fact does not prove, however, that Paul did not believe in the existence of these things. At the same time it

[263] 2 Thes. 1 :7-10.

does prevent us from affirming with certainty
that he did.

It is likewise with regard to the Judgment.
Paul is strikingly indefinite touching the details
of it, as compared with the Synoptic Gospels.
He gives no descriptive scene of that event.
Whether or not he thought of it in the way in
which it is pictured in the Gospel narratives it is
impossible to say.   There can be no question as
to his firm belief in the fact of the Judgment.
He repeatedly speaks of it, sometimes representing God as Judge,[264] at other times Christ.[265]   In
one case he seems to pass imperceptibly from the
one to the other.[266]   In this particular passage
moreover it is evident that the Judgment takes
place at the time of the Parousia, and it is an
important part of that event.   Just as we have
seen that Christ at his coming will bring from
the abode of the dead those who are asleep in
Jesus and transform those of his faithful ones
who are alive at his coming, so at his coming
he will destroy those who are not his.   Looked

[264] Rom. 2:2-6; 3:5, 6, 19, 20; 14:10.
[265] Rom. 2:16; 1 Cor. 4:5; 2 Cor. 5:10.
[266] 2 Thes. 1:5-10.

at in the light of their cosmic significance, the two acts are really one. They both constitute the Redeemer's triumph over his cosmic enemies. The believers he rescues from the abode and power of Death. The sinners are destroyed. God gave these sinners the opportunity to prepare for the day of wrath, but they refused to take advantage of the salvation provided in the gospel. They in consequence failed to provide for themselves escape from the .rath of God, since they did not become his sons, receive his Spirit and partake of his nature.

If one desires to penetrate more deeply Paul's thought touching the Parousia, the Resurrection, the Judgment and the destinies of the saved and the unsaved, he must study these questions in the light of the contemporary religious thought of Paul. Jewish apocalyptic presents many parallels.[267] The large part which was played by eschatology in the mystery-religions of the Græco-Roman empire in this period, as well as in other forms of religious expression, makes it probable that Paul's thought on these problems

[267] Bousset, *Die Religion des Judentums*, 2 Aufl., Berlin, 1906, 294 ff., 308 ff., 474 ff.

of the future would find expression in forms which were intelligible and agreeable to his auditors. That this was the case we have indirect evidence in the fact that these problems of the future seem not to have been the basis of controversy. Some members of the Corinthian church, how many we do not know, had doubts regarding the resurrection. Paul's reply to their questionings indicates that these skeptics were not a menace to the church, as though they were propagandists, having the denial of the resurrection as one of their chief tenets. The Thessalonians had questionings regarding those who had fallen asleep, and also perhaps regarding the time when the Parousia would take place. But this only goes to show how fully they accepted the doctrine of the Parousia, and presumably all that went with it in Paul's preaching. For it was to these Thessalonians that Paul wrote reminding them how they had turned from idols to serve a God living and true and to wait for his Son from the heavens.[268]

The probability is that the absence of detailed statements regarding such important facts as

[268] I Thes. 1:10.

the Parousia, the Resurrection, the Judgment and the future state of the good and the evil finds its explanation to a great extent in the fact that these ideas encountered little opposition from those to whom Paul preached. In many quarters, both among Jews and Pagans, men were endeavoring to flee from the wrath to come. To a considerable degree that was the unifying religious thought of the time. If we are right in giving to Paul's idea of salvation a dynamic and cosmic significance, then we may say with considerable probability that Paul found a ready response to his eschatology among the common people of the Græco-Roman empire, both Jews and Pagans, for demonology was common among both classes.

Regarding the destiny of the believers we have already spoken in Chap. II.[269] It remains only to observe that in contemplating the glorious future which awaits the faithful, Paul expresses himself with moderation and reserve. One has only to compare the Pauline epistles with the Book of Revelation, or with the extra-canonical apocalyptical writings to be impressed with this

[269] Pp. 33-48.

fact.   The apocalypses make much of the external features of the blessed state, what might be called its materialistic aspect.   They give elaborate descriptions of the city beautiful, with its street of gold, gates of pearl, etc.   They portray the appearance of the redeemed, whom the writers have seen in vision, showing how, when transformed, they may be mistaken for superior beings.   The angelic choir, the great white throne, the elders, the beasts, the book of judgment, the Lamb slain from the foundation of the world—all these are set forth before the reader in graphic detail.   Paul on the contrary makes no use of such materialistic representation. He appears to be concerned not with the environment of the redeemed but with their actual condition or state.   He sums up this in two general expressions—glory and conformation to the likeness of Christ.   This conformation to the likeness of Christ in particular means assimilation to the nature of God, who becomes all in all.   This stands for the completion of the cosmic cycle.   Men, or certain of them, were ordained from the first by God to attain to this cosmic oneness with God.   This marks the completion of

the cosmic cycle. The cosmic conflict comes to
an end. God's enemies are all subdued. Harmony and peace pervade the universe. The
dualism gives place to a divine oneness, which is
God.

SELECTED BIBLIOGRAPHY

BAUR, F. C. *Das manichäische Religionssystem,* Tübingen, 1831.

GFRÖRER, A. F. *Das Jahrhundert des Heils,* Stuttgart, 1838.

HILGENFELD, A. *Der Galaterbrief,* Leipzig, 1852.

LIPSIUS, R. A. *Die paulinische Rechtfertigungslehre,* 1853.

Zeitschrift f. wiss. Theologie, 1858, 1860, 1866.

MORISON, JAMES. *A Critical Exposition of the Third Chapter of Paul's Epistle to the Romans,* London, 1866.

WEISS, B. *Lehrbuch der bibl. Theologie des N. T.* Berlin, 1868. 7 Aufl., 1903. Eng. trans., 1888.

LIGHTFOOT, J. B. *St. Paul's Epistle to the Galatians,* London and Cambridge, 1869.

SCHÜRER, EMIL. *Lehrbuch der neutestamentlichen Zeitgeschichte,* Leipzig, 1874. 2 Aufl., *Geschichte des jüdischen Volkes im Zeitalter Jesu Christi,* Bd. I, 1890; II, 1886; 3 und 4 Aufl., Bd. I, 1901; 4 Aufl., Bd. II, 1907; III, 1909.

HOLSTEN, C. *Das Evangelium des Paulus,* Berlin, 1880.

WEBER, F. *System der altsynagogalen Theologie,*
Leipzig, 1880. 2 Aufl., *Jüdische Theologie,*
1897.

KLÖPPER, ALBERT. *Der Brief an die Colosser,* Berlin, 1882.

SPITTA, FRIEDRICH. *Der zweite Brief des Petrus
und der Brief des Judas,* Halle, 1885.

EVERLING, OTTO. *Die paulinische Angelologie und
Dämonologie,* Göttingen, 1888.

GUNKEL, HERMANN. *Die Wirkungen des heiligen
Geistes,* u. s. w., Göttingen, 1888.

HOLTZMANN, H. J. *Hand-Commentar zum Neuen
Testament,* Freiburg, 1889. 2 Aufl., 1891, 1892.

DEISSMANN, ADOLPH. *Die neutestamentliche Formel "in Christo Jesu,"* Marburg, 1892.

CHARLES, R. H. *The Book of Enoch,* Oxford,
1893. 2d Edition, 1912.

KABISCH, RICH. *Die Eschatologie des Paulus,* Göttingen, 1893.

SANDAY AND HEADLAM. *A Critical and Exegetical
Commentary on the Epistle to the Romans,*
New York, 1895.

HOLTZMANN, H. J. *Lehrbuch der neutestamentlichen Theologie,* Freiburg und Leipzig, 1897.
2 Aufl., hrsg. von A. Jülicher und W. Bauer,
Tübingen, 1911.

WERNLE, PAUL. *Der Christ und die Sünde bei
Paulus,* Leipzig, 1897.

SIEFFERT, FRIEDR., *Meyer Kritisch-exegetischer Kommentar über d. N. T. Der Brief an die Galater.* 9 Aufl., Göttingen, 1899.

WEISS, B., *Meyer Kritisch-exegetischer Kommentar über d. N. T. Der Brief an die Römer.* 9 Aufl., Göttingen, 1899.

CHEYNE AND BLACK. *Encyclopedia Biblica,* New York and London, 1899-1903.

WERNLE, PAUL. *Die Anfänge unserer Religion,* Tübingen und Leipzig, 1901. 2 Aufl., 1904. Eng. trans. of 1st Edition, *The Beginnings of Christianity,* 2 vols., New York and London, 1905.

BRÜCKNER, MARTIN. *Die Entstehung der paulinischen Christologie,* Strassburg, 1903.

VOLZ, PAUL. *Jüdische Eschatologie,* Tübingen und Leipzig, 1903.

Zeitschrift f. d. neutestamentliche Wissenschaft, 1903, 1905.

BOUSSET, WILHELM. *Die Religion des Judentums,* Berlin, 1903. 2 Aufl., 1906.

WREDE, W. *Paulus,* Halle, 1904. Eng. trans., *Paul,* London, 1907.

SCHMIDT, CARL. *Koptisch-Gnostische Schriften,* Leipzig, 1905.

ZAHN, THEODOR. *Kommentar zum Neuen Testament. Der Brief an die Galater.* Leipzig, 1905.

SMITH, W. B. *Der vorchristliche Jesus,* Giessen, 1906.

WEISS, JOHANNES. *Die Schriften des Neuen Testaments,* Göttingen, 1906-7. 2 Aufl., 1908.

BOUSSET, WILHELM. *Hauptprobleme der Gnosis,* Göttingen, 1907.

JÜLICHER, ADOLPH. *Paulus und Jesus,* Tübingen, 1907.

MEYER, A. *Wer hat das Christentum begründet, Jesus oder Paulus?* Tübingen, 1907. Eng. trans., *Jesus or Paul?* London and New York, 1909.

DEISSMANN, ADOLPH. *Licht vom Osten,* Tübingen, 1908. 2 u. 3 Aufl., 1909. Eng. trans., *Light from the Ancient East,* New York and London, 1910.

BAUER, WALTER. *Das Leben Jesu im Zeitalter der neutestamentlichen Apokryphen,* Tübingen, 1909.

BURTON, E. D., SMITH, J. M. P., AND SMITH, G. B. *Biblical Ideas of Atonement,* Chicago, 1909.

CLEMEN, CARL. *Religionsgeschichtliche Erklärung des Neuen Testaments,* Giessen, 1909. Eng. trans., *Primitive Christianity and Its Non-Jewish Sources,* Edinburgh, 1912.

DIBELIUS, MARTIN. *Die Geisterwelt im Glauben des Paulus,* Göttingen, 1909.

DOBSCHÜTZ, ERNST v., *Meyer Kritisch-exegetis-*

*cher Kommentar über d. N. T. Die Thessa-
lonicher-Briefe,* 7 Aufl., Göttingen, 1909.

GRANBERY, J. C. *Outline of New Testament
Christology,* Chicago, 1909.

WEISS, JOHANNES. *Paulus und Jesus,* Berlin, 1909.
Eng. trans., *Paul and Jesus,* London and New
York, 1909.

FEINE, PAUL. *Theologie des Neuen Testaments,*
Leipzig, 1910. 2 Aufl., 1911.

REITZENSTEIN, R. *Die hellenistischen Mysterien-
religionen,* Leipzig und Berlin, 1910.

WEISS, JOHANNES, *Meyer Kritisch-exegetischer
Kommentar über d. N. T. Der erste Korin-
therbrief.* 9 Aufl., Göttingen, 1910.

ZAHN, THEODOR. *Kommentar zum Neuen Testament. Der Brief des Paulus an die Römer.*
1 u. 2 Aufl., Leipzig, 1910.

WEINEL, HEINRICH. *Biblische Theologie des Neuen
Testaments,* Tübingen, 1911. 2 Aufl., 1913.

CASE, S. J. *The Historicity of Jesus,* Chicago,
1912.

INDEX OF SCRIPTURE REFERENCES

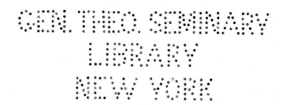

THE following pages contain advertisements of a
few of the Macmillan books on kindred subjects

NEW BOOKS ON RELIGION

The Development of the Christian Religion

By Shailer Mathews, Author of "The Church and the Changing Order," "The Gospel and the Modern Man," etc.   Cloth, 12mo. $1.50 net.

Dr. Mathews here enters upon the little explored territory of social theology.   His general position is that the scientific theologian should approach his task through the social sciences, particularly history, rather than through philosophy.   The main thesis of the book is that doctrines grow out of the same social forces as express themselves in other forms of life.   Dr. Mathews finds seven creative social minds and treats the development of the various Christian doctrines as they have emerged from the earlier of these minds and must be created by our modern social mind.   Such a treatment of Christian doctrine serves to make theology a vital rather than a merely scholastic or ecclesiastical matter.   The study of the social minds of the past, with their creative influence on Christianity, gives a point of view for the study of the intellectual needs of today's religion.   This volume conserves the values of the religious thinking of the past, and is, in addition, a positive force in the reconstruction of the religious thinking of the day.

The Christian Life in the Modern World

By Francis G. Peabody, Author of "Jesus Christ and the Social Question," etc.   Cloth, 12mo.

The purpose of this book is to meet the increasing impression that Christian idealism is inapplicable to the conditions of modern life and to indicate the terms and conditions on which these ideals may be perpetuated.   There are chapters on The Practicability of the Christian Life, The Christian Life and the Modern Family, The Christian Life and the Business World, The Christian Life and the Making of Money, The Christian Life and the Using of Money, The Christian Life and the Modern State and The Christian Life and the Christian Church.

PUBLISHED BY
THE MACMILLAN COMPANY
64-66 Fifth Avenue
New York

NEW BOOKS ON RELIGION

Modern Religious Movements in India

By J. W. FARQUHAR.
Illustrated. Cloth, 8vo. $2.50 net.

This comprehensive survey of present day religious tendencies in India is of tremendous importance and significance to every student of religion. In it are described the various new religious organizations which, under the impact of the West, have arisen in India during the past century. The Brahma, Prarthana, Arya, and Deva Samajes, the Ramakrishna Movement, Theosophy, the Bharata Dharma Mahamandal, the Caste and Sect Conferences, the Social Reform Movement, and the efforts of Muhammedans, Parsis, Jains and Sikhs to accommodate their systems to the needs of modern times are all dealt with in turn. Portraits of the leaders are included in the volume. The original basis of this work is the Hartford Lamson Lectures on the Religions of the World, though in its printed form the material has been revised and enlarged.

Vital Elements of Preaching

By ARTHUR S. HOYT, Professor of Homiletics and Sociology in Auburn Theological Seminary, and Author of "The Work of Preaching" and "The Preacher." Cloth, 12mo. $1.50 net.

The Work of Preaching, one of Dr. Hoyt's former books, deals with the sources and formation of the sermon for the present age. The Preacher, still another of his works, places emphasis upon a vital spiritual personality in giving the message. This volume touches the temper of the man both as to the truth and the lives of his hearers. "Preaching," writes Dr. Hoyt in his preface, "is a social virtue. Nothing can be more fundamental to the preacher than his humanity. The deepest needs and desires of the age must be felt in his life if his word interprets aright the gospel of the new man."

The author here discusses the psychology of preaching, though without formal and philosophic analysis. He always has in mind the question, How shall we speak so as to help men into the largest life?

PUBLISHED BY

THE MACMILLAN COMPANY

64-66 Fifth Avenue
New York

Social Christianity in the Orient: The Story of a Man, a Mission and a Movement

By JOHN E. CLOUGH. Written down for him by his wife, EMMA RAUSCHENBUSCH CLOUGH. Illustrated. Cloth, 12mo. $1.50 net.

" The Christian world was thrilled over thirty years ago by the story of Dr. Clough's work. Now for the first time we have opportunity to study his methods, to get at the social, economic and religious principles which lay behind it."—W. H. Faunce, D.D., *President of Brown University.*

"Dr. Clough was one of the founders of the modern era in missions. Before him the purpose largely had been to produce a western type of Christianity in Oriental lands. Dr. Clough caught a vision of the transforming of peoples. Upon the foundation of the crude village organization which he found he built a Christianity of Oriental type. His method of baptizing converts from heathenism, thousands at a time, on credible profession of faith in Christ, has profoundly affected the methods of Christianity in India and other lands. In this book we have a graphic description of his ideas and methods and experiences."—E. F. Merriam, D.D., *Managing Editor of the Watchman-Examiner*

The Gospel of Jesus and the Problems of Democracy

By HENRY C. VEDDER, Professor of Church History in Crozer Theological Seminary and Author of "Socialism and the Ethics of Jesus." "The Reformation in Germany," etc. Cloth, 12mo. $1.50 net.

"We need a reconstructed theology. The theology of all churches has been dominated by monarchical ideas; it needs to be recast in the mould of democracy; it has been permeated with ideas of social privilege such as were unfavorable when aristocracy ruled the world; it needs to be restated in terms of equal rights." These sentences from Dr. Vedder's preface at once show his viewpoint. The Gospel and the Awakening Church, The Problem of Social Justice, The Woman Problem, The Problem of the Child, The Problem of the Slums, The Problem of Vice, The Problem of Crime, The Problem of Disease, The Problem of Poverty, The Problem of Lawlessness—these are the topics of the ten chapters. The book is undoubtedly one of the most important contributions to the study of present day religion that has yet been published.

PUBLISHED BY

THE MACMILLAN COMPANY
Publishers   64–66 Fifth Avenue   New York

NEW BOOKS ON RELIGION

The Man of Nazareth

By FREDERICK L. ANDERSON

Cloth, 12mo, $1.00 net

This is a study of the life of Christ written not for theologians, but for the average man and woman. The most important problems about Jesus and his career and the conditions of his time are related with a simplicity that will commend the book to those who find so much of religious writing vague and unsatisfactory. Dr. Anderson has not sought to solve disputed questions, but rather to present in a clear light the broad and generally accepted facts of the Saviour's life, and while there is no ponderous show of learning the volume is undoubtedly the result of many years of hard study and application to the subject.

Live and Learn

By WASHINGTON GLADDEN

Cloth, 12mo, $1.00 v :

An exceedingly practical little book is this one in which the distinguished clergyman and writer seeks to impress upon his readers the necessity of getting possession of themselves. Learning how to see, how to think, how to speak, how to hear, how to give, how to serve, how to win and how to wait — these are the author's themes. The chapters are interesting because of the happy fashion in which Dr. Gladden clothes his thoughts ; they are valuable in that they contain the wise counsel of a mature mind in which are arranged and stored the products of a long experience. The work is especially suited to young people — of the high school age, for example. It will assist them to obtain and maintain a proper adjustment toward life. It will, however, be read with no less profit by all whose minds are open, who are willing to learn, whether they be sixteen or sixty.

THE MACMILLAN COMPANY

Publishers   **64-66 Fifth Avenue**   **New York**